100 Happy Naked New Yorkers

100 Happy Naked New Yorkers

by Kiana Tower

Writers Club Press
San Jose New York Lincoln Shanghai

100 Happy Naked New Yorkers

Writers Club Press
an imprint of iUniverse, Inc.

For information address:
iUniverse, Inc.
5220 S. 16th St., Suite 200
Lincoln, NE 68512
www.iuniverse.com

This book contains discussions of sex.

ISBN: 0-595-23895-5

Printed in the United States of America

To the people of the City of New York—the toughest, kindest, most fascinating people in the world

Contents

Acknowledgements

This book would not have been possible without the help of all the New Yorkers who freely gave me their time, their feedback, and most importantly, their true stories about the singles scene in New York.

I'd also like to offer special thanks to three people who were a huge help and inspiration to me: Cindy Adams, Neil Cavuto, and Craig Newmark.

Cindy Adams—Thank you so much for writing about me in your column—twice! In March of 2002, my first book had just come out. Brrrring! Phone rings and a voice on the other end says: "Please hold for Cindy Adams." **The** Cindy Adams, I wonder? A moment later, your voice comes on: "Dear, what's this book of yours all about? Folks doing it all over the Bay area in unusual places. Up against copy machines and such? What is going on?" The blurb you wrote in your column was very funny. Then, in June of 2002, you encouraged your readers to participate in the research survey for this book. I received a huge jump in responses! What a fun and fascinating group of readers you have. Some of the stories were too hot to print! (But, I sure enjoyed reading them.) The rest of the stories are included in this edition of the book. Thank you Cindy. You've been a huge help.

Neil Cavuto—I did a lot of radio and TV interviews while publicizing my first book, but none were as fun as appearing on "Your World with Cavuto." Thank you for the invitation, and for the kind words on my book. You're a class act, and as I watch your show now, from the comfort of my home, I always wonder if the guests are having as much fun as I did that day.

Craig Newmark—founder of "craigslist" (**www.craigslist.org**). The online communities of craigslist have been incredibly supportive in the creation of both my books. Over half of the research subjects in both my books came from craigslist. Craigslist is a unique place on the web, filled with intelligent, down-to-earth people. Thank you Craig for creating such a wonderful online community where we can all connect!

Last, but not least, a big thank you to the support system upon which I anchor my emotional stability. Thank you to my girlfriends in the Bay area for encouraging me to write, and helping me come up with the theme for the first book. (Yes, DebSue, Amy, Christine and Susan.) Thank you to Kirsten Carrazzone in New York for making everyone she knows buy my first book. Thank you to my husband for not only helping with the baby, but even doing my share of the chores, so that I could have more time to write. You are my rock. And, thank you to my parents and my three big brothers for always loving me just as I am.

Introduction

Why write this book?

In January of 2002, I published "Sex in Silicon Valley," a saucy, scandalous, research-based book about the dating woes of Bay Area geeks. The book achieved some modest success. Not enough to tempt me to quit my day job, but enough to inspire me to write a second book. I set out with the intention of expanding my research area, and writing a sequel that encompassed funny true stories of dating woes all over the United States.

But, during the spring of 2002, the plan changed. As my first book began to rise in the sales rankings on Amazon.com, I noticed a fascinating trend. Folks on the East Coast, and New York in particular, were showing more interest in the book than folks in the Bay Area. My best newspaper write-up appeared in a NYC paper, and my most prominent TV interview took place in New York.

So, I posted a few notes on electronic bulletin boards, feeling out the idea of doing a sequel based solely in New York. New Yorkers loved the idea and immediately began volunteering themselves (and their hapless friends.) Encouraged, I began collecting research surveys in early May 2002. Within five weeks, I had more than enough material for a book. I went through the surveys, and chose the 100 best surveys to be the basis of this book.

And…New Yorkers do love talking about sex! Some survey respondents provided so much material that I could have written a whole chapter on them alone.

How was the research conducted?

I got the word out about the book through New York-specific Internet bulletin boards, such as craigslist, Yahoo!, and Salon.com's personals. I invited New Yorkers to sound off with their opinion in a 20-question survey, hosted off of my existing website, **www.sexinsiliconvalley.com**. I was impressed with the naked honesty, and the intelligent responses, I received. Thank you to all the New Yorkers who participated in the research.

"New York" versus "New York"

I was born and raised in New York. When I make this statement to friends here in California, they assume I spent my childhood dodging taxi cabs in the heart of Manhattan. Not so. I was born in Westchester, raised in Putnam, and went to college someplace way upstate. All part of New York. For the purposes of this book, the term "New York" is used to mean either "New York City" or "New York State." The majority of the survey respondents are NYC residents, but there is some representation from folks in the suburbs, and tri-state area.

Gay?

Once I'd finished the draft of this book, I asked (OK, begged) several of my friends to proofread it. One of my proofreaders sent back the following comment: "After each person's quote, you have this blurb telling their age, their sex, and where they are from. I also want to know if they are straight or gay. I spent a lot of time re-reading trying to figure out the he's and she's..."

There are some terrific stories submitted by gay New Yorkers. Eight percent of the survey respondents are gay. So, the gay survey respondents are noted in their blurb after their info. Ex: *Draven, a 24-year-old gay female from the suburbs.*" If it doesn't say "gay," you can safely assume the survey respondent is talking about their adventures with the opposite sex.

A Note About Pennames

I allowed all of the survey respondents to be completely anonymous, and asked them to choose a penname. I thought they would choose normal sounding pennames such as "Bob" or "Lizzy" or "Claire." But alas, in a result very reflective of the online age that we live in, many of the pennames came out sounding more like online user IDs, or perhaps even the crew roster of a starship: Cendrillon, Fishbulb, etc. Perhaps I should have explained the concept of a penname? Ah, but in the end, I just decided to leave the pennames as is. Since we all spend so much time in the online world, I suppose we're all used to folks with names like Cendrillon and Fishbulb anyway…

What You are About to Read

The book is a combination of fun and serious topics, all focused on dating and relationships in New York. On the side of fun, I've got irreverent and saucy topics such as "What's the most unusual place you've had sex?" and "East Coast sex versus West Coast sex." On the more serious side, I spoke to New Yorkers about the emotional aftershocks of 9/11, and how this has affected their relationships. It would be impossible to capture every nuance of the city. Think of this book as a snapshot in time, capturing the musings of 100 New Yorkers in the spring and summer of 2002.

Email me. Yelling at me is OK, too.

What do you think of this book? Love it? Hate it? Go ahead and email me, even if it's to yell at me. (Hey, my first book wasn't always universally loved. I enjoy a bit of controversy.) Have ideas for future research projects? Email me at **KianaTower@aol.com**.

Wanna' read some freebies? Even as I head to press, more surveys are still popping into my emailbox. So, as surveys come in, I'll pick out the juiciest stories and post them on my website. As always, there is no charge or fee for pulling writings off the website. I've also been toying with the idea of doing a general sequel covering the whole U.S. The project is tentatively titled "More Sex in Silicon Valley—and other great places." Wanna' be in the book? Come take the survey. You can find it all at **www.sexinsiliconvalley.com**. Enjoy!

1

Dating in New York: "Terror Sex," 9/11 and Other Tales

One evening in early May, as I was printing out all the surveys that had popped into my email box over the course of the day, I noticed a survey respondent had written: "Terror sex was overrated." I made a note in my notebook: "Terror sex?"

Soon, more surveys started referencing "terror sex." I researched the term. After the events of 9/11, folks started having sex as if their lives depended on it. And, the sex was incredible. Sex with friends. Sex with strangers. Sex with people who had similar experiences that day. After so much death, everyone wanted to be reassured they were still alive. They searched for life in the most elemental way possible. The French call an orgasm, "le petit mort," the little death. Through sex, New Yorkers began to search for life.

The survey respondents spoke of many different aftereffects of September 11th. Some survey respondents wrote of the romance having "gone out of life" and being "too upset to have sex." Others experienced prejudice where they hadn't before. Fourteen percent of survey respondents felt 9/11 had a negative impact on their relationships and social lives.

But, almost one-third of respondents felt the singles scene in New York had changed for the better. People started reaching out more to others. For some, sex was easier to get. Some sought out old loves, and patched up troubled relationships. Others decided it was time to seek out Mr. or Ms. Right.

The research for this book was conducted in May and June of 2002. For some, the impact of 9/11 is still being felt intensely. For others, life has now taken on new pleasures. Read on, and appreciate the diversity of New Yorkers, in their own words.

Life is fragile. Live out your fantasies.

"At first, we didn't have much sex because we almost felt guilty. So many people were in agony that we didn't feel right enjoying ourselves. But, after awhile, we started having more and frequent encounters in more ironic situations…the realization that life is fragile and limited came into effect, so we try to live out all of our fantasies."—*Urban Metaphor, a 22-year-old male, originally from Tennessee*

"There is an increased sense of urgency now when I have sex. There are more feelings attached to it. I feel like I am riding a wave."—*Tracy, a 30-year-old female, originally from Connecticut*

Live for the moment

"People seem to be more willing to take chances and live for the moment." *Footman, a 41-year-old male, born and raised in New York*

The luck of the Irish?

"After 9/11, the social scene was muted for a while. But, once the initial shock wore off, there was one group of folks that was getting really lucky. Firefighters and police are getting a lot more ass. They're like celebs. The entire FDNY must have gotten lucky on St. Paddy's Day. Good for them. They deserve it." *Rico, a 23-year-old male, born and raised in New York*

No more bullsh*t

"Since 9/11, I've found that men are more willing to actually believe in living for the moment…and as a woman who lives by that creed, it has meant that more men are willing to dive into relationships with more honesty than before. It's as if no one really wants to waste time on bullshit. If you want a quick hook-up and nothing more, then that is what you advertise. I mean, even in a dating situation, while the two of you are feeling each other out and talking, I find that the conversation is much more upfront than before 9/11. No one is offended by being direct." *Camila, a 35-year-old female, born and raised in New York*

"There is definitely a sexual after-effect from 9/11. There is much more openness amongst people in general. I'm with the same girlfriend I was with then, and we definitely have sex more now than before. Something about 'seize the moment,' I guess."—*Bateman, a 25-year-old male, originally from New England*

Karma, ultimate orgasm and terror sex

"9/11 tested the strength of a nation, but even more so, the resiliency of New York. I work in the financial district. I saw the entire events of 9/11 unfold right before my eyes. I saw the towers fall. I lost a friend. I ran down 30 flights of stairs just in time. I felt completely and utterly alone in a city full of people. I was one of the 'post 9/11 clingers.' I ended up having phenomenal sex with a mere stranger. We met at an East Village bar during the days after 9/11 when downtown was sealed off and my company was out of an office. We clung to each other a couple more times, trying to make a 'relationship' happen, then realized we are who we are, New Yorkers in search of the perfect mate in a not-so-perfect city."—*Kaitlyn, a 23-year-old female, originally from New Jersey*

"I've had a great deal more partners since 9/11. Everyone seems to be trying to reach out to everyone. Right after it happened, I had comfort sex. Folks now are calling that terror sex. I just needed to feel the comfort of another human being. I needed to feel like I was still alive. It made things easier."—*Dylan, a 23-year-old male, originally from the Midwest*

"Terror sex was way overrated."—*Norm Penn, a 35-year-old male, born and raised in New York*

"I think people realized for a while that the only thing that really matters in life is love. People sought out that love and passion. The sex was a release from the loneliness people felt."—*Jack, a 26-year-old male, originally from Miami*

"9/11 affected every person around. But sex is something that takes you away from all that. If there's karma, there's ultimate orgasm."—*Aquarius, a 49-year-old female, born and raised in New York*

"9/11 didn't change sex or dating for me at all. Although, a few of my friends made full use of 'terror sex', i.e. let's make love not war, now, before anything else happens."—*LondonMan, a 30-year-old male originally from England*

I just don't want to be alone

"At first it seemed to open things up a bit, and maybe there is a continuing sense of openness and a desire to be with someone else, rather than just living and working alone. In hindsight, the experience is still a maze to me."—*Nick, a 44-year-old male, originally from Arizona*

I don't believe in terror sex

"I don't understand how there could be a connection between 9/11 and sex. Based on the widely disparate levels of education and maturity in this city, it would be difficult to form a consensus connection. Many people in America don't even understand what provoked 9/11. Moreover, they lack the desire to understand the Middle East , its cultures, and how it shapes the thinking of its inhabitants."—*BudFox, a 26-year-old male, originally from Boston*

A French phone call ruined the mood

"I have not experienced 'terror sex.' One time, my girlfriend came over for sex. My sister in Paris called. She made some snide remark about September 11th. It got me so upset that my girlfriend had to leave in the same condition she came."—*Blav, a 47-year-old male, originally from upstate New York*

Mr. or Ms. Right, where are you?

"The devastation of the attacks, and the subsequent economic landslide, seemed to throw everyone into 'hyperdrive' searching out Mr. or Ms. Right."—*Little Fifi, a 28-year-old gay male from upstate New York*

"I am making an effort to go out more. I'm really putting myself out there, and I'm more willing to take chances. I'm sure there is a man out there for me, and I'm more determined than ever to find him."—*BlackBarbie, a 25-year-old female, born and raised in New York*

"9/11 made me think more about romance, rather than just searching for great sex. I have been a single career woman, and I thought that was all I ever wanted to be—that career would be enough for me. After 9/11, I started to think more about marriage and having a family of my own. Sex for sex's sake just doesn't seem as important anymore."—*Roxy, a 33-year-old female, lives in the suburbs*

"I think people have been trying to get closer. More people are finding themselves ready to settle down with long-term partners and single people are now looking for someone to be there, a partner. No one really wants to be alone anymore."—*Betty, a 28-year-old female, born and raised in New York*

A dry spell

"I had a long dry spell, then finally in February, I felt ready to begin dating again."—*Francisco, a 27-year-old male, originally from California*

A dry spell, then out of control

"For a few months after 9/11, I was very unsexual. However, after the New Year, I became out of control in seeking casual sex. I think I was trying to get human contact in any way that was possible."—*Cowboy, a 22-year-old gay male, originally from Kansas*

More sex, and a marriage proposal

"Since 9/11, I've definitely had more sex. I've also had ex-boyfriends calling and saying they are sorry and to forgive them. And, I've had one marriage proposal!"—*Brooklyn, a 31-year-old female, born and raised in New York*

We can work it out

"At the time of 9/11, my boyfriend and I were broken up. But since then, we are trying to work it out, and get back together."—*Cindy, a 28-year-old female, originally from Michigan*

Being Jewish, Being Muslim

"I dated a Catholic girl for four months after 9/11, but it didn't work out. I'm sure that 9/11 had its effects, because I am a Muslim. She never could be sure how she felt about me. Our relationship was impacted by being from different backgrounds, different social circles, and the anti-Muslim prejudice."—*Tolga, a 27-year-old male, originally from Turkey*

"9/11 has given my worst paranoia justice. I choose mates based on how they would deal if there were another bombing, or a bio-attack in town. Or, if folks starting targeting Jews again, but this time in New York, instead of Tel Aviv or Berlin. (I am Jewish.)"—*Norm Penn, a 35-year-old male, born and raised in New York*

A shared experience

"Now we have all have something in common. There is always something we can talk about together. If you are stuck in a conversation, all you have to say is: 'So, where were you when it happened?' Instant conversation. Having this shared experience has improved things for me.'"—*Matthew des Jardins, a 23-year-old male originally from New Mexico*

Promiscuity

"Since 9/11, it's become much easier to meet people. Promiscuity is on the rise."—*Deliboy, a 31-year-old male, born and raised in New York*

The age factor

"I can understand where the question comes in when you're asking about 9/11. The tragedy has affected everyone. But, it's much more so for those who are older, and single, and suddenly realized they are alone. At my age, we bounce back pretty quickly."—*Potion, a 21-year-old female, born and raised in New York*

Changed perspectives

"Before 9/11, I'd been playing it kind of fast and easy, as I was both dating someone, plus still seeing other people. Once the event happened, I sought out the person I was dating, and we left the city for a week. During that time, we decided to commit ourselves totally to our relationship and make it work. Life just took on a different meaning. Sure, it hasn't been easy giving up the singles lifestyle, but 9/11 helped put life in perspective and now I appreciate the simple things we have together."—*Zander, a 35-year-old gay male from Connecticut*

Aftershocks

"Due to stress, my boyfriend and I broke up. He's a NYC cop who couldn't address his feelings and I couldn't bare to watch him struggle and not let me in. We are still trying to work through it all."—*Princess of NY, a 24-year-old female from the suburbs*

"Life has been better since the post-traumatic stress has gone away. Initially, I was dating someone whom I'd been trapped in the World Trade Center with. I was injured and needed a lot of help to escape. Our connection was obviously exacerbated by the fact that we'd gone through this shared experience together. 9/11 made everything happen in an intense way."—*Olive, a 36-year-old female, born and raised in New York*

WTC—excuses?

"I worked in the World Trade Center. It seems, like I knew it would, that things are back to normal. This isn't such a good thing. People used and still use 9/11 for all kinds of excuses and sympathy that they should not."—*Dust, a 33-year-old male, born and raised in New York*

Sleep with me—I work at Ground Zero

"I slept with a World Trade Center worker. At least he said he was, but I never heard from him again. I think he was taking advantage of the whole thing."—*New to the City, a 24-year-old female, originally from Baltimore*

The jumpstarting of the biological clock

"The events of 9/11 made my biological clock start ticking. It's time for me to settle down and get married. Maybe NYC will not be here if I wait too long."—*Ace, a 35-year-old male from the suburbs*

Hiding. Unable to orgasm.

I work in a 9/11-related job, and I've become more tense and stressed. I'm more interested in spending quiet time alone at home than going out and hooking up. I have ended a couple of hook-ups at the last (worst) possible moment because I just couldn't relax and 'let go.'"—*Alice, a 23-year-old female, originally from North Carolina*

Hiding and bitter

"I didn't go out socially or speak to anyone new at all for months. I'm bitter."—*C.L. a 35-year-old male, originally from Brazil*

I was gone; now she's gone

"I was in love with this woman before 9/11, but I was out of town for four weeks when it happened. When I came back, she felt differently, and everything had changed for her."—*Lance, a 30-year-old male, originally from Minnesota*

Coffee? No? Still, no?

"The frequency of girls that I meet has not changed. I'm not rushing into bed any faster either. Girls don't seem to be more willing to go for coffee with me, if that's what you're asking." *Gavin, a 25-year-old male, originally from England*

Reach out and sleep with a genuine New Yorker

"I've had more experiences with people visiting NYC wanting to sleep with me."—*New York Romeo, a 32-year-old male, originally from the mid-Atlantic*

A kinder, gentler city

"9/11 has made me more aware of people, friends and family. Life is fragile, and we are here for only a short and troubled time. 9/11 brought out the best in most people. Almost everyone helped out and did more than usual for people they didn't know. I was proud to be a transplanted New Yorker and glad to help in anyway I could."—*The Kissing Bandit, a 52-year-old male originally from Boston*

"The people you meet are much nicer, calmer. The mad people got madder, and the nice people got nicer, but overall, we are all trying to work together now."—*Melanie, a 21-year-old female, originally from Pennsylvania*

Enough!

"The events of 9/11 have made me more sexually aware. I am more aware of each moment. But, I am so sick of hearing some of the comments people make about 9/11. If I hear: 'I thought I had seen it all, and then came 9/11' one more time, I think I might shoot myself."—*Henry Paul, a 27-year-old male, originally from upstate New York*

Where's all that great sex gone?

"I've only had sex ten times since 9/11. That's really bad. I usually have it much more than that. Sex in my home would be nice sometime soon…please."—*Fishbulb, a 28-year-old male, originally from Florida*

The 5 night one-nighters

"For the first weeks post 9/11, everyone was a lot more mellow. Guys wanted to hang out for longer periods of time…the one-daters turned into 4-5x daters. Everyone wanted someone next to them at night. Now, it's mostly fallen back on the way it was."—*Kaitlyn, a 23-year-old female, originally from New Jersey*

A sense of normalcy has returned

"My girlfriend broke up with me right after September 11th. It was horrible for a bit. It seemed trivial to want to go out and meet someone when the country is on the verge of war. But, after a few months, I met someone, and now, I've found happiness again."—*Draven, a 24-year-old gay female from the suburbs*

"Well, 9/11 made my relationship more secure. We realized how valuable it was to have the other person there for us. Overall, while we miss the Towers, the dating scene remains unchanged. What has changed is people are living fuller, richer lives. (Heck, I'm in law school which was a direct result of my reaction to what happened on 9/11.) Perhaps people who were thinking of leaving unfulfilling relationships have done so and are now out looking for their true loves. But, for many people, it's business as usual. I just attended a party that was in an apartment literally overlooking Ground Zero. People partied, flirted and hooked up as though Ground Zero didn't exist at all, and it was actually adding to the lighting scheme of the scene."—*Trez, a 36-year-old female, originally from Minnesota*

◆   ◆   ◆

Sounding off on 9/11

I offered the survey respondents a chance to sound off on the events of 9/11, outside of their dating lives. Here are their responses:

A jittery, nervous city

"New Yorkers are jittery and nervous since 9/11."—*Sky Ace, a 25-year-old male from the suburbs*

Last one out, turn off the light.

"There seem to be more people I know talking more seriously about living somewhere else. Not a lot of people I know have really acted on the idea, but there is now the idea that there could be 'life outside Manhattan,' especially by folks overwhelmed by 9/11 and feeling the threat of more to come."—*Nick, a 44-year-old male, originally from Arizona*

Lost my job and my home in just a few hours

"The effects of 9/11? Well, good question. I worked at the World Trade Center and lived 4 blocks away. In a matter of hours, I lost my job and my home. Getting laid off when you are homeless is kind of hard. I'm hanging in there, though."—*Rico, a 27-year-old male, originally from Dallas*

All our skins became 'American'

"It was nice for a while that the skin of other cultures living inside the United States had just become 'American.'"—*Che, a 29-year-old male, born and raised in New York*

Let go. Move on.

"I think it's time that we all let go and move on."—*MonkeyBoy, a 30-year-old male, originally from Texas*

These terrorists have female issues

"I think that if terrorists were able to make friends with women, communicate with them, and have mutually satisfying sex with them, they would do a lot less killing. A lot less killing of each other, and a lot less killing of us. I think they are repressed, and repressive. 9/11 has convinced me that their way of life is a real drag, with nothing constructive to offer. The positive aftereffect of 9/11 is that I feel more blessed than ever. I feel wealthy. 9/11 opened my eyes. Living in an open culture is such a great thing! And, it is so rare."—*Norm Penn, a 35-year-old male, born and raised in New York*

A not so happy birthday

"Well, September 11th is my birthday, so that day has sort of forever been ruined for me."—*NYLivin, a 27-year-old male, originally from Hollywood*

The appeal of out-of-towners

"I think it's a goddamn shame, this '9/11' business. I have noticed that experienced New Yorkers often go for out-of-towners, or foreigners, in the hope that they haven't been 'ruined' yet."—*Blav, a 47-year-old male, originally from upstate New York*

2

What's the Most Unusual Place You've Had Sex?

New Yorkers are creative when it comes to finding unusual places to make whoopee. Sometimes their creativity is motivated by necessity—too many roommates, unaffordable hotels, long drives back home to the 'burbs. Suddenly, parks, subways, doorways, restroom stalls and taxicabs take on a new appeal.

Read on, and appreciate the innovation of New Yorkers in their native habitat. The survey question that generated these responses was: "What's the most unusual place in New York you have ever had sex?"

"Yoo hoo! Taxi!"

After living in California for several years where everyone drives their own cars, (even if it means sitting in traffic jams six lanes wide,) I'd forgotten how much of New York life takes place in taxis. And apparently, having sex in a taxicab is something of a required ritual for NYC residents.

"In a taxi. I unzipped. She gave me oral. Happens all the time in NYC."—*Raymond, a 41-year-old male, originally from California*

"Most unusual place I've had sex? It was in a taxi, after we had just left a bar, and were going down a dark street. I think all the cars around us got a good show, as well as the cabbie."—*Tracy, a 30-year-old female, originally from Connecticut and Boston*

"Not very original from a NYC perspective, but I like doing it in the back of a taxi cab while riding through Central Park."—*Longhorn, a 33-year-old male, originally from Houston*

"My best time was in the backseat of a cab, with a very randy date. My date jumped on top of me and started riding me. We gave the driver a free show, and a nice tip. He didn't seem to mind."—*Joe, a 31-year-old male, born and raised in New York*

"I did it in the backseat of a taxi, but I'm not sure for a New Yorker that is the least bit unusual."—*Colleen, a 28-year-old female, originally from Michigan*

"Oral in a taxi. I had a girlfriend who was very uptight, except when it came to taxis."—*New York Romeo, a 32-year-old male, originally from the mid-Atlantic*

"My girlfriend gave me oral in a taxicab on the Prospect Expressway."—*Blav, a 47-year-old male, originally from upstate New York*

I am trying and trying to picture this but not having any success...

"In a taxi cab. I dated a guy who was pretty 'big' and I didn't have to lay flat in the backseat. He was long enough that he could reach to penetrate."—*Dee, a 38-year-old female, originally from Puerto Rico*

Calling Clark Kent

"I dated a guy for many years who had an obsession about sex in phone booths. It didn't really work (it did for him, but I didn't exactly get fully satisfied, if you know what I mean). My other unusual place was a taxicab. I did this many, many times. It was great. It was a lot of fun because it felt 'forbidden'—like Dad was in the front seat. I did that for 11 or 12 years before I developed a conscience about how what I did affected others. I have a lot of respect and appreciation for the drivers who just let it all happen without kicking us out onto the street and throwing my clothes out after me."—*Trez, a 36-year-old female, originally from Minneapolis*

The tube and the doodle

"I have received oral sex (my doodle was satisfied) on a late night subway."—*Mr. Far Side, a 23-year-old male, originally from Long Island*

```
Note from the author: I think it's adorable that you call it
your doodle.
```

"I did it on the #5 train heading downtown, late one night."—*Joe, a 31-year-old male, born and raised in New York*

"My most unusual place? A subway station closet."—Boo Boo, a 29-year-old female, born and raised in New York

This could really drive usage of public transit!

"Well, the vibrations of a NYC commuter bus drove me to pleasure myself before reaching work."—*Aquarius, a 49-year-old female, born and raised in New York*

Ahoy!

"My most unusual spot was on the deck of the Intrepid during a fundraising event."—*Knacka, a 27-year-old male, born and raised in New York*

Good things come in threes

"I've had a couple of unusual places. There was the woods in front of Manhattan College, bare ass to the ground. There was the bathroom of a club, oh, and a stairwell for that matter." *Yoon, a 43-year-old male, born and raised in New York*

"I have three good ones to share. 1) the dressing room of Joan & David. 2) the Suffern Thruway rest stop parking lot, and 3) a corn maze in Stone Ridge while wearing a button-front denim skirt. Yes, I was wearing a skirt."—*Little Fifi, a 28-year-old gay male from upstate New York*

Poor lady probably thought she was about to get mugged…

"I met a man for a drink. We liked each other instantly and felt the familiar stirrings of lust. We found a deserted stairwell near the Westside Highway, and did it right there. Just hiked up my skirt. Just as we were about to finish, there's this old lady walking her dog, not more than 20 feet away. I laughed out loud at the incongruity of it all, and then, we both climaxed. Noisily. We didn't mean to be quite so noisy, but it just happened that way. The old lady looked right over to where we were, alarmed. We ducked down, butt naked, onto the cold concrete. She and her little dog quickly walked away. She probably thought she was about to get mugged!"—*Camila, a 25-year-old female, born and raised in New York*

The fine universities of New York

"It was 9:30 PM, after my MBA class. I was a teaching assistant, so I had keys to the professor's office. Everyone went home, except for this girl I liked. We ended up going back to the professor's office, and we did it right there on his desk. The experience was so good, that we repeated this throughout the semester. Like 10 times in all. It was one of the highlights of my education and made being a teaching assistant totally worthwhile."—*Tolga, a 27-year-old male, originally from Turkey*

"I was working with a girl who was interning at a magazine. One night, we went out with a group of people. We hit it off, and wanted to do something about it. But, she lived in an NYU dormitory and all her dorm mates were home. It was 2 a.m., and we needed to go someplace, anyplace. So, we trolled around the corner to the laundry room of her NYU dorm. There was a camera there, so we carefully positioned ourselves out of sight of the camera. I unzipped my pants, lifted up her skirt, and we had sex standing right there in the laundry room."—*Fishbulb, a 28-year-old male originally from Florida*

Play ball!

"Yankee Stadium baby! Rain delay, upper deck. And, I think the fact that you know there are so many people watching you just made it that much more exciting."—*Princess of NY, a 24-year-old female from the suburbs*

A room with a view

"A girl I was dating had just moved into a new building that was still under construction. We made our way into the unfinished, penthouse apartment. We had sex against the glass with a great view of the Upper West Side."—*MonkeyBoy, a 30-year-old male originally from Texas*

Note from the author: I'll bet the Upper West Side had a great view, too.

"I had sex in the conference room of my 30th floor office. The only thing is, I didn't realize until after the fact that the people in the building next to mine saw the entire thing. Things were a bit awkward for a while."—*Kaitlyn, a 23-year-old female, originally from New Jersey*

"I had sex in the middle of a living room with six huge glass windows and no shades. It was across the street from the Chelsea Hotel. Anyone above the third floor in the hotel could have watched us for about two hours."—*2Extreme, a 27-year-old male, born and raised in New York*

"In a hotel. That's not so unusual but our 'audience' was. The two security guards were watching us from a ladder outside of our window. We did not notice them until I got up to open the window when we were done, (I was sweaty,) and we saw two dudes hauling ass down the ladder and running. The room was free after a phone call to the front desk with a description of the guards."—*Rico, a 27-year-old male, originally from Dallas*

Goin' Clubbin'

"An S&M club in the Village with this chick I took out a couple of times. It was exciting. She was a real exhibitionist! The adrenaline rush made it sexy."—*BudFox, a 26-year-old male, originally from Boston*

"I once did it with a boy in the three-foot gap between the DJ booth and the men's bathroom wall at Roxy on a Saturday night. We didn't finish, because after five minutes, we had drawn quite a crowd. There were three or four shirtless party boys whacking off while watching us. We eventually quit because our audience was beginning to draw unwanted attention from the club staff. Pretty hot, though. I've also scored in alleyways south of Canal Street, and in both Central and Prospect Parks."—*Tiger, a 26-year-old female, originally from Iowa*

"It was in the couples room of an S&M club. My boyfriend and I went to this club because we kept hearing how funny it was, and how interesting. We saw transvestites, old people going at it, and all sorts of other really weird stuff. We went upstairs to the couples only room where the scene was more voyeuristic. I sat on his lap and we had sex on a chair. The whole experience was very interesting."—*Betty, a 28-year-old female, born and raised in NY*

Uh…I don't think you'll find your doggie in there…

"My most unusual place was in a park under the George Washington Bridge. It was the summer of 2000, and I ran into a woman that was looking for her dog. I told her I would help her find it. After an hour of searching in unusual places, like the bushes, we agreed we need a break. We sat down in the green lawn area. She said she felt tense from losing her dog. I told her that the dog would come back in time, and that she needed to release some energy. She made some heavy eye contact with me, so I kissed her. And the next thing I knew we were getting hot and heavy right there in the green lawn area!"—*Sky Ace, a 25-year-old male from the suburbs*

Well…it makes those long meetings go by much more quickly…

"I work in publishing. I once had sex right on the conference room table of a major magazine company."—*Rebecca, a 29-year-old female, originally from Boston*

Bathrooms—not just for tinkling anymore

After reading these stories, I'm no longer going to assume strange sounds in a public restroom means someone's suffering intestinal distress…

"I have had sex in virtually every top restaurants' bathroom, from Aquavit to Zarela's."—*Bateman, a 25-year-old male from New England*

"I did it with a girl in the bathroom of a very busy restaurant/bar. Someone could have walked in at any moment!"—*Deliboy, a 31-year-old male born and raised in New York*

"It was in the bathroom of a very upscale restaurant, which shall remain nameless. Our poor waitress kept going back to our table looking to take our order. But, we were otherwise occupied."—*Melanie, a 21-year-old female, lives in the tri-state area, originally from Pennsylvania*

"I was at Spa on a Thursday night. Thursday night is gay party night, which is cool, since I'm gay. Then, a very odd thing happened. There was this beautiful woman, and I found myself very attracted to her. I ended up taking her to the woman's bathroom and we did it right there in one of the stalls. It was great, although very surprising!"—*Cowboy, a 22-year-old gay male, originally from Kansas*

"My most unusual place? Well, just the normal spots for a New York-ers. The roof of my apartment building. Central Park. The restrooms at the Four Seasons. The restroom at Club Macanudo, and of course, the restroom at El Cid."—*Mary, a 36-year-old female, originally from Texas*

Man's best friend? I'm assuming this means doggy style?

"A lavatory at the Empire State Building. Yeah, the sinks are great to hold onto during man's best friend."—*JujuBee, a 30-year-old female, originally from California*

Ah, the sand, the surf, the little fishies

"I did it at Jones Beach, in the water, while it was packed with people!"—*Potion, a 21-year-old female, born and raised in New York*

That nice park by the big statue of the green lady

"I did it at Battery Park, on a park bench in the early 90's."—*Ellie, a 34-year-old female, born and raised in New York*

Columbus Circle

"On a bench at Columbus Circle with a girl I knew from years ago. We just met on the street and did it."—*Dust, a 33-year-old male born and raised in New York*

Bear Mountain

Bear Mountain is a scenic state park, nestled along the Hudson River, so-named because the profile of the mountain resembles a bear lying down. Although, it seems bears aren't the only ones lying down there these days.

"It was at Bear Mountain on a Sunday afternoon. Ah, the great outdoors!"—*Jack, a 26-year-old male, originally from Miami*

"The most unusual place that I've ever done it is on the side of Bear Mountain, on a blanket. We were in the middle of the woods. A deer came right up to our blanket! Several people passed within eyesight, but they saw we were otherwise occupied, and they moved on. We were naked the whole day, enjoyed a picnic lunch, and each other, all day long. It was a beautiful, and delicious, day!"—*The Kissing Bandit, a 52-year-old male originally from Boston*

The greatest park of all—Central Park!

"It was Central Park at a Simon and Garfunkel Summer Concert. I made out with a sexy and mellow girl for 3 hours. She sat on me and I hugged her. She was 21 and visiting the States from Northern England…a real hot lover. I sure wish I had her address."—*Ace, a 35-year-old male from the suburbs*

"My most unusual place? Central Park! I still smile every time I walk by there."—*Ralph, a 24-year-old male, originally from South Jersey.*

"Mmmmmm…I did it in Central Park."—*NYC Boy, a 36-year-old male, born and raised in New York*

"Besides the typical spots, such as the bathrooms at bars, the Bloomingdale's dressing rooms and on 7th Avenue in Chelsea, my overall favorite was on a sunny weekend afternoon in Central Park. I was seeing this gorgeous guy. We stopped in the middle of our jog, and ended up totally nude, and went at it. People stopped to watch." *Zander, a 35-year-old gay male, originally from Connecticut*

"The most unusual place for me was in a playground. Me and my boyfriend at the time had a few drinks, went out rollerblading at night and ended up in the park with our rollerblades still on, having sex standing up."—*Dee, a 25-year-old female, originally from upstate New York*

And, just south of the park…

"One night, after a party, I was walking my date home on 59th Street, just south of the park. We started making out and I couldn't contain myself. I hiked up her skirt, pinned her to the wall, and started touching her in all the right places. Her response drove me crazy. I told her: 'We need to take care of this right now!' She was willing. Before I knew it, I had lifted her up and over the wall, into the park. I made passionate love to her, while we both got covered with dirt and leaves. The next day, with a wry grin, she showed me her scuffed knees."—*Dylan, a 23-year-old male, originally from the Midwest*

Quack, quack, quack

The Roslyn Duck Pond is a reserve in Long Island. Not too reserved, apparently…

"My most unusual place was right next to the Roslyn Duck Pond."—*Norm Penn, a 35-year-old male, born and raised in New York.*

This is the dawning of the age of Aquarius

"I was hanging out with my best friend at a bar, and we met these two adorable young guys. They both worked at the Teddy Roosevelt Mansion in Oyster Bay. They asked us if we wanted a private tour of the mansion. It was very beautiful, but also very creepy at night. We ended up coupling off, and each going into bedrooms to make love. I was making out, really hot and heavy with my guy, when I sensed there was a being around us. The wood floor started creaking. I got very scared and felt someone was in the room with us. Even though I was really scared, I wanted to finish, so we did. It was an unreal and spooky sexcapade though."—*Aquarius, a 49-year-old female, born and raised in New York*

Oh, any doorway will do

"I'm partial to abandoned doorways."—*Meg, a 22-year-old female, lives in NYC*

Seems only fair to try before you buy

"My most unusual place was at Lord and Taylor, in the bedding department, on a bed."—*Jocko, a 70-year-old male, originally from Memphis*

From a stuffy man partial to museums

"I don't know if having sex in an unusual place is any different than doing it anyplace else. Nor do I know how many normal people spend time looking for unusual places (it has always seemed a bit of a fetish to me.) I have had sex, not by design but by the effects of lust, in a stairwell, on a rooftop, and in a secluded part of the Metropolitan Museum."—*Nick, a 33-year-old male, originally from Arizona*

Auto erotica?

"Outside my parked car on Riverside Drive. Anyone could have seen us! That's what made it so great!"—*Bobby, a 37-year-old male born and raised in New York*

Feel that funky music...

"Inside the DJ booth at Webster Hall (a club in the Village)."—*Jones, a 26-year-old male, born and raised in New York*

To the roof!

"On top of a roof in Chelsea, under the stairs, where anyone in the buildings that rose above us could watch in full detail."—*Lance, a 30-year-old male, originally from Minnesota*

"The rooftop!" *Frub, a 31-year-old male, originally from upstate New York*

"On the roof of my boyfriend's apartment building. There was a beautiful view of the Empire State Building. It was in the summer and we laid a blanket down and went at it. Unfortunately, the blanket was not sufficiently padded and I bruised my tailbone pretty badly. It was definitely worth it, though."—*Micro Bee, a 27-year-old female, originally from San Francisco*

"I lost my virginity on the rooftop of the building where I used to live as a teenager. It had just rained so the roof was wet. We put a jacket down and did it. It was very clumsy and quick."—*Brooklyn, a 31-year-old female from Brooklyn*

"It was on the rooftop of my old apartment building during a thunder-and-lightning storm. The roof was rubberized with sealant, so I felt quite safe from death, but scared at the same time. I lay on my back and rain fell into my eyes."—*Jessica, a 28-year-old female, originally from New Hampshire*

Like playing with fire, do you?

"Silly 'ol me. I did it with the girlfriend of an NFL wide receiver in her apartment."—*Lewis, a 22-year-old male, originally from Philadelphia*

But alas, still hoping and wishing...

"I truly wish I could have sex someplace really thrilling. The best I could do was to get my girlfriend to have sex out on our fire escape. It was hot and raining that day. We couldn't resist climbing out the window, and enjoying the feeling of the hot rain against our bodies."—*Urban Metaphor, a 22-year-old male, originally from Tennessee*

"Nowhere unusual yet, but give me some more time!"—*Snippity, a 24-year-old male, originally from California*

"None yet! But now, you've inspired me to have such an experience. I'll work on it!"—*Matthew des Jardins, a 23-year-old male originally from New Mexico*

Snippity and Matthew, you come up with something really good for me, and I'll consider putting it in a sequel. I mean really good, OK?

3

Dating Disasters in New York

We've all had them—horrifying blind dates, dates you wish you could forget, dates you have forgotten that you wish you could remember. Whoever said 'misery loves company' must have been talking about dating disasters. As these stories prove, we're all in this together.

DWD (Dating While Drunk)

"I once got drunk, and forgot what my date looked like. Or, rather, there was another girl in the place that was strikingly similar to my date, I guess."—*Knacka, a 27-year-old male, born and raised in New York*

"I met a girl and we went out on a first date. I had too much to drink and blacked out. When I was supposed to meet her for a second date, I couldn't remember what she looked like."—*Bateman, a 25-year-old male from New England*

Out of respect for my penis

"My biggest dating disaster happened recently. I met this woman online. We seemed to hit it off, and agreed to meet in-person. So, we met. The problem was, she wouldn't stop giggling. Like I would say one word and she would bust out laughing. I went to the bathroom to see if I had a booger hanging out or something. I didn't. Anyway, she said she's never had sex. Amazingly, she invites me back to her apartment about 10 minutes later. When I walked into her apartment, her bed was right by the door, there were condom wrappers on the floor, and a gigantic box of condoms, right next to the bed. A virgin? I don't think so! Needless to say, out of respect for my penis, and to keep it clean and unharmed, I found some great reason why I had to leave immediately."—*Rico, a 27-year-old male, originally from Dallas*

Just walk away

"I haven't really had any dating disasters. If the date turns sour, I just walk away. There are so many more dates to be had in this city! So many successful women to meet!"—*Matthew des Jardins, a 23-year-old male, originally from New Mexico*

Hello, Rebecca?

"I was dating a guy named Gary for nearly three months. He was actively pursuing me, but I kept trying to keep things casual. We started seeing each other about 3 or 4 times a week, but we never went back to his place, always to mine. At the end of the third month, I get a phone call at 7:30 in the morning. 'Hello, is this Rebecca?' says the voice on the other end. 'Who's calling?' I ask. 'Hi. This is Ally, Gary's girlfriend. Is he with you? I was wondering if he had our keys on him. I locked myself out and I wanted him to come by and let me in.'"—*Rebecca, a 29-year-old female, originally from Boston*

Busted!

"My worst dating disaster happened just last night. I was out with a girl I'd been dating a while, and we sat down in a movie theater right next to a girl I'd just asked out the night before."-*Dylan, a 23-year-old male, originally from the Midwest*

But, I only married her for a green card! That doesn't count as married!

"Does the time a girl left at 2 a.m. because she found out I'd married a friend five years ago to help with her green card count?" *C.L., a 35-year-old male, originally from Brazil*

Blind dates and online disasters! Aaaaah! The agony!

"Just about every blind date I've been on is at least mildly disastrous."—*Dino, a 41-year-old female, born and raised in New York*

"A friend set me up on a blind date with a foreign guy who only knew three words of English: I love you. All night long, he kept saying 'I love you, I love you.' Besides the fact that we could not communicate, he was a sore sight. I haven't been on a blind date since then."—*Dee, a 25-year-old female from upstate New York*

"I met a really nice guy over email. We didn't exchange pictures, though, and agreed to meet on a blind date. It was a nightmare. He had brown teeth."—*Cendrillon, a 29-year-old female, originally from France*

"My worst dating disaster? That's easy! I met someone over the Internet. We wrote back and forth for several weeks, but never spoke over the phone. Her name was Chris. She was ready to meet me, but just didn't want to talk on the phone. So, we decided to meet at a diner, and if she liked the way I looked, she would just walk on over. I waited an hour. Nothing. I had just ordered myself a slice of pie, when a young man came up and sat alongside me at the counter. He said hello, and we made small talk for a few minutes until I was done eating. I was just getting ready to leave when he told me he was Chris. All along, I had been assuming 'Chris' was a woman. I ran out of the diner and didn't look back."—*The Kissing Bandit, a 52-year-old male, originally from Boston*

"I met someone online and thought I really liked him. But, when I met him in person, I totally decided I didn't like him. So, I just bolted out the door and left. Of course, here in New York, you see everyone all the time if you have unresolved issues with them…so now I see him everywhere."—*Cowboy, a 22-year-old gay male, originally from Kansas*

Coitus interruptus

"I was making out with a girl in her family's apartment. She was 16 and I was 17. Her mother comes home from work early at 3 PM, and catches us in a bedroom…all nude and lewd. I looked at the girl's mom and said. 'Good evening." The mom turned snow white, turned around, and walked out the front door. We both got dressed, split the building rapidly, and went to park under the George Washington Bridge. We sat there drinking a bottle of red wine to mellow our nerves. Her mother later talked to her about what had happened. Her daughter told her to get back into the 1990's sex scene for the now generation. I'm just glad her mother didn't walk in when we were smoking a joint a 12 noon!"—*Ace, a 35-year-old male from the suburbs.*

All tied up and nowhere to go…

"I met up with a guy at a gay bar. He asked me back to his place. He tied me up, but the stuff he did after that just didn't really get me excited. So, I didn't, um…react. He must have gotten mad because he just left me there tied up. After a while, he finally untied me and asked me to leave."—*Sam, a 25-year-old male, born and raised in New York.*

Missed connections

"I inflicted my worst dating disaster onto myself. I lost the phone number of a girl that I really, really, really liked. She wanted me to call her for a second date. I never could find her again. I think she really liked me, so I hope I didn't hurt her feelings. I was depressed for weeks, and hunted all over the city for her."—*Urban Metaphor, a 22-year-old male, originally from Tennessee.*

"I met a girl at Macy's. She was a perfect 10! She agreed to go out on a date with me, but she never showed. Where did she go? Where are you?"—*Sky Ace, a 35-year-old male from the suburbs*

Office romances (and other ways to get slapped with a sexual harassment suit)

"I once fell for someone in my office, and it was deliciously mutual. She commenced sending me steamy Instant Messages, and I considered her my girlfriend. Then, she started to get cold feet, but she didn't let me in on it. She started to express her doubts to a colleague, who advised her to take the situation to Human Resources. My girlfriend dumped me out of the blue, warned me not to stalk her, and then a few weeks later, I was fired without explanation. I'd say we had a communications issue."—*Norm Penn, a 35-year-old male, born and raised in New York*

The Atkins diet, martinis and Prada shoes

"No major dating disasters, but I can think of two semi-disasters. The first one was meeting someone who turned out to be a dork (met him on a flight, wasn't nearly as attractive on the ground.) I was on the Atkins diet so I had to drink a lot of martinis (I'm a rules girl.) The next day he called about 5 times as I was trying to sleep off the wretched hangover. Over the next couple of weeks, he proceeded to call like 30-50 more times. I stopped answering my phone. After I was certain he had gotten the message, I started answering my phone again. Alas, he called one night, got through to me, and started talking like nothing ever happened. My response was 'hey, I'm really glad you called. There is something I wanted to talk to you about. I'm not interested in dating you and I would appreciate it if you never called me again.' He finally took the hint.

My only other incident that I would classify as being on the disastrous side happened right after I'd just had the best date ever. We had a midnight dinner, sex all night, sushi for breakfast, a dance around Prada in the shoes I wanted to buy, and sex before the long goodbye. I was certain we were a match made in heaven, but alas, he never called me after that day. I was heartbroken. I still don't know where I went wrong."—*Trez, a 36-year-old female, originally from Minnesota*

Ooooh, you're fugly

"I agreed to go furniture shopping with a guy I met the night before at Central Park. He said he needed to furnish his seemingly perfect Murray Hill pad (then again, I was there at 4 a.m., who knows what it really looked like in the daylight.) Never do furniture shopping with guys who you barely know…he was a total fugly (yes, f***ing ugly) dude. Now, if I hadn't been so drunk the night before, I would've realized this. And, he was an arrogant, touchy jerk. I left him in the middle of Chelsea to furniture shop on his own. The only thing was, I had his cell phone in my bag and had to eventually drop it off at his apartment where he told me I was a selfish, spoiled bitch. Yeah, well, at least I'm not fugly."—*Kaitlyn, a 23-year-old female, originally from New Jersey*

A plumber, a dildo and a l'il woman

"I met a guy through an online personals network. On our first date, he tried to convince me to dress as a plumber or a handyman, strap on a dildo, and then go to his female sex slave's apartment unannounced, try to get her into bed, and then take pictures of the whole thing. Remember, this was on our first date! I didn't know the guy, or his girl. Needless to say, I ended the date pretty quickly. I still run into him from time to time, though…and his l'il woman. She looks pretty sub-dued and miserable."—*Tiger, a 26-year-old female, originally from Iowa*

Those potent mixed drinks at Benihana's

"After a very nice dinner at Benihana, I went for drinks with a guy. We were getting along so well that I wasn't paying attention to how much I was drinking. I guess I must have done too many shots. On the way home, I passed out in his car before he could even close my door. Half-way home, I woke up and puked all over the side of his car. I was barely able to give him directions to my house. The worst part was that he called the next day. I mean, do I really want to be involved with a guy that calls a girl that pukes a all over his car?"—*Princess of New York, a 24-year-old female from the suburbs*

Note from author: Well, Princess, you can conclude one of two things. Your date was either very desperate, or, he was a true gentleman. Your call.

Hershey—the great American chocolate pants

"Well, my dating disaster is more funny than serious. Early in my time here in New York, I went to pick up a blind date via taxi. I was wearing my nicest new white pants, with a blazer and tie. I actually sat on a melted Hershey bar that had been left on the taxi seat. I didn't notice anything at first, but once folks started looking at me funny, I figured something was amiss, and there was this big blotchy brown stain all over my bottom. Fortunately, my date turned out to be really cool, and we were able to laugh about it. I don't wear white pants at all any-more."—*Nick, a 44-year-old male from Arizona*

He slept with me, and then turned gay

"I just found out that my recent ex-boyfriend is gay. I'm very discouraged about the dating scene, so now I just bop 'em and leave 'em."
Dirty Dee, a 38-year-old female, originally from Puerto Rico

Emotional baggage, anyone?

"I met a girl at a party, but she had a boyfriend. A few weeks later, I found out from the host of the party that she and her boyfriend have broken up. I got her number, called her and she agreed to dinner. We had a great dinner, and then went bar hopping. All night long, we enjoyed each other's company, and had genuinely good conversation. When we arrived back at her apartment, she invited me in. One thing led to another, and we ended up with our clothes off, making love. First, we did it in the living room, then, we did it again in her bedroom. Exhausted, I fell asleep in her bed. About 2 a.m., I awoke suddenly as my date leapt over me, and jumped out of bed. I looked up, and saw a dark shape in the bedroom doorway, approaching us quickly. It was her ex-boyfriend, and he looked really, really pissed! I jumped up, and the ex-boyfriend and I looked at each other, eye-to-eye. I was much taller, and he must have reconsidered beating the crap out of me, because he looked away from me, and told the girl he wanted to talk to her in the living room. As soon as they left, I quickly started throwing my clothes on, getting ready to bail out of there. Next door, the two were crying and carrying on. I was just about to leave, when the girl returned. 'Why are you leaving?' she asked. I said: 'Are you kidding me?!' and I took off. As I left the apartment building, there was the ex-boyfriend sitting on the steps, head in hands. I was a little worried he might be waiting to kill me. No, he was simply crying. I apologized to him, wished him well, and took off for the nearest bar. It took several stiff drinks to calm my nerves."—*BudFox, a 26-year-old male, originally from Boston*

Herpes is just not sexy

"No major disasters, but I did go out on a date with a woman who turned out to be a professional dominatrix. I had another date with someone who was infected with Herpes. This put a quick end to any physical component of the date."—*2Extreme, a 27-year-old male, born and raised in New York*

"Honey, you can do better!"

"I met a very sexy, masculine (but un-stylish…you know the type) man at a bar. He was a cop from Weehawken, New Jersey. We exchanged phone numbers. He called a few days later; and we went to the Townhouse Restaurant. Right from the beginning, he was a control freak. While we were being seated, he grabbed me by the elbow and propelled me through the dining room. Over dinner, he proceeded to drink to excess and verbally abuse the restaurant staff. He treated me like a 'bimbo' with huge fake breasts and high heels and frosted blonde hair! At one point he went to the bathroom, the two old gay men at the next table leaned over and said to me, 'Honey, you're too pretty to have to put up with him!' I was mortified! Later, back at the bar, he kept trying to undress me, (loosening my tie, pulling my belt off) all the while telling me how big his penis was. At one point, he grabbed my hand and made me feel his member through his pants. (Yes, it was huge, but that's beside the point!) As we left the restaurant, I said thank you and good-bye, and tried to gracefully exit the scene. He followed me, saying we should go to a hotel to have sex, and that I should pay for the room. I ignored him, and headed for the nearest cab. He kept following me. He yelled that since he had paid for dinner and drinks, that I should at least put out. He said nobody ever turns him down for sex! I hopped into the cab. He was yelling, trying to open the door, and banging on the cab window. I ordered the cab driver to 'GO!' and we sped off. Now, I know what it feels like to be a woman! Jeez!"
—*Michael B., a 33-year-old gay male, born and raised in New York*

Truck, please!

"I had a disastrous date with a girl from New Jersey. After 10 minutes, I wanted to push her in front of a truck. After 15 minutes, I wanted to jump in front of a truck."—*Raymond, a 41-year-old male, originally from California*

Boring!

"I had a blind date with a Wall Street type. He clearly thought I would be riveted by hearing him recount the minutia of his day. After the entrée, and before dessert and coffee, I pleaded a headache and left."—*NYCKnows, a 35-year-old female, originally from Houston*

What was I thinking?!

"I've had one night stands that still make me feel disgusting when I think about them. One was after just an hour of knowing a guy I met in a bar. Ugggh!"—*Meg, a 22-year-old female, originally from Boston*

Perhaps you should save the "phone people" comment for the end of the date...

"I met this great girl at a bar one night, and we made out right there at the bar. She gave me her phone number, and over the next week, we had some great conversations over the phone. The following Friday, we went out to dinner, and I planned on going to a comedy club after. Somewhere between the main course and the check, I said: 'Maybe, we're just phone people.' She took it the wrong way, and left."—*Lance, a 30-year-old male, originally from Minnesota*

Alas, I was a fool.

"I've brought on my own disasters when I've tried to date too many people at once. Here's a tip—don't write about your sexual encounters with other men in your journal, and then forget to put your journal away when your boyfriend comes over…But that wasn't my biggest disaster. I once had a dinner date with a good guy, and I thoughtlessly stood him up so that I could have sex with a guy that turned out to be a real rotten loser. I just left the good guy waiting at the restaurant for me, while I had sex with this man who was no good for me. The good man, the one I'd cuckolded, threw a loud fit in the hallway of my building at 4 AM. He proved to have a most colorful vocabulary. My roommate and neighbors were about to wring my neck. I think someone finally called the cops. Poor guy. It was totally my fault, and there was nothing I could do to make it right with him. All for a disastrous tryst with a loser!"—*Jessica, a 28-year-old female, originally from New Hampshire*

Stalkers, Serial Killers and Borderline Psychotics

"I was sitting on this girl's bed, waiting for her to finish her telephone session with her shrink (who was in L.A.). She was out on the terrace, not realizing she'd left the window open. It was only our second date, but she was talking about me in a way that made me realize she was very possibly a serial killer." *LondonMan, a 30-year-old male, originally from England*

"I met someone at a social event, and we started dating. Then, he went psycho. He started calling me ten times a night, leaving weird messages. I finally broke the ties. He had a very tough time dealing with the fact I was breaking up with him. Now when I see him in public, I ignore him like he doesn't exist."—*Brooklyn, a 31-year-old female from Brooklyn*

"I met a guy at work. I thought he was cute, so I started to pursue him. It turned out he is a psycho stalker. I had to change jobs."—*Boo Boo, a 29-year-old female, born and raised in New York.*

"I once dated a stripper, and she started stalking me! I don't recommend dating strippers."—*NYC Boy, a 36-year-old male, born and raised in New York*

"I once dated a psycho who insisted that I love her. OK, 'insisted' is too weak of a word. She was borderline psychotic!"—*Fishbulb, a 28-year-old male, originally from Florida.*

4

Gay in New York

New York has a thriving, vocal gay community. It's a great city to be gay and single, for both men and women. Eight percent of the survey respondents were gay, and some wrote such comprehensive survey responses that I could have devoted a chapter to each one of them.

On June 6, 2002, Cindy Adams was kind enough to mention my research efforts on this book in her daily column. Within hours, my emailbox was flooded with new surveys. As I read through them, I noticed that many of the surveys were from gay men. Cindy seems to have a very strong following in the gay community, and these men had some exciting stories to share. Even older gay men participated in the survey. Jocko is a 70-year-old gay male, originally from Memphis, who enjoys having sex in the Lord and Taylor bedding department. CBrown is a 71-year-old gay male, who enjoys a good romp at the beach.

Here are true stories of the gay and lesbian scene in New York. If you'd like to read more about these swinging singles, more gay and lesbian quotes are included in many of the other chapters of this book. (Hey, this is an equally opportunity sex book.)

Bathroom erotica

"I have always had more sexual encounters in NY compared to anywhere else. People tend to be less inhibited here. I once had a really hot encounter in the bathroom of a bar. Girl walks in while I'm washing my hands and pushes me against the wall and kisses me. I kissed her back. Some people walked into the bathroom, so we headed to a bathroom stall, and pleasured each other in there, with more privacy."—*Draven, a 24-year-old gay female from the suburbs*

So easy to find sex here! (stories from young men from Kansas)

"Sex in the gay community is so easy to find. There are so many opportunities to have sex in the city—websites, clubs, sex clubs, the gym, walking on the street, subways, and parks. I could have sex every night if I wanted to."—*Ike, a 26-year-old male, originally from Kansas*

"Sex in New York is great! It can be totally spontaneous—you walk down the street, make eye contact with someone, and then end up in the bathroom of a nearby coffee shop. Or, you can also meet amazing people and have intense, meaningful relationships. It's all available here."—*Cowboy, a 22-year-old gay male, originally from Kansas*

Lovable and 95

"I've found no shortage of gay men here in New York—both upstate, and here in New York City. I'm just a little 95 pound guy, but I've found all manner of lovable men wanting to date me!"—*Little Fifi, a 28-year-old male from upstate New York*

Oh, but the Muscle Mary's!

"The toughest part is finding gay men that are men…these Muscle Marys are all women!"—*anonymous comment from a gay male.*

Sticky roof tar

"My most unusual encounter was on a hot summer night in the East Village. My boyfriend and I went up to the roof of his apartment to smoke a joint. An hour later, he had sticky roof tar all over his back!"—*Patrick, a 42-year-old male, born and raised in New York*

Gay bars, and...

"I had just gotten free of a bad three month relationship, and I was ready to have some fun. Fun found me! I was standing in a gay bar with friends, and a good-looking man walks in. 'Hi!' I said, before he was even totally through the door. He came over, and we started talking. After an hour of talking, he said he had to go. I asked if he wanted company. I walked him home, and for my trouble, he gave me oral right in the doorway of his brownstone apartment house! It was just what I needed!"—*Michael B., a 33-year-old gay male, born and raised in New York*

...naked gay bars

"I had the most amazing experience at a gay bar. A naked gay bar. You were required to check your clothes at the door. I walked in there wearing just a smile. It took no time at all before I found some people who wanted to have fun. I ended up tied to a pole, and had...well, fun. It was the most amazing night!"—*Sam, a 25-year-old gay male, born and raised in New York*

The pleasure of a good car ride

"A few days ago, I picked up a guy on the Internet. He was from Westchester. I didn't feel like going all the way back to his place, and I didn't want to take him back to my place. So, we ended up having an encounter, right in his car on a side street in the West Village. People were walking right by us and didn't even know what was going on. It was very erotic!" *Ike, a 26-year-old male, originally from Kansas*

Zander offers his viewpoints on being gay in New York

Zander is a 25-year-old gay male who submitted an extensively filled out research survey, with detailed answers on every question. Here's Zander, in his own words, giving a comprehensive rundown of the gay singles scene in New York.

"Gay life in NY is fun and exciting. This city is packed full of gay and bi men!" says Zander. "But, there are downsides. Commitment is not respected very much. Guys will make a pass at you, even if they know you're in a committed relationship. And, once you do commit your-selves, it's a struggle to avoid temptation. So many men to tempt you here! The gay men here are attractive, in-shape and ethnically diverse. Plus, the men here are willing to try new things. They're not virgins. Typically, the New York gay male has had numerous partners, and is experienced in how to provide pleasure. They're not repressed about any style, position or location for getting together. And, how many places can you literally meet someone on your way to work, take them someplace discreet place, have sex, and do it all over again during your lunch hour?"

"For a gay man, it is much easier to get a date here than in other areas of the country," writes Zander. "Gay life is more accepted here, and there are more options. I love Latin men, and have plenty of choices here. Although, sometimes it's tough to find someone who truly wants a date, and not just sex at the end of the night. (But I do love that too.)"

"My biggest dating disaster? It was with a hot, supposed 'executive' from The GAP. After taking me to a lame restaurant for bad food, we went to a club to go dancing. My date said he had to go to the bath-room and disappeared for quite a while. I ended up heading to the bathroom, too, and there I caught my date screwing an ex-boyfriend of mine! I literally caught him inside my ex. I decided then that the night was over for me," says Zander.

Zander concludes with the following bit of advice: "The single's life is fun, and I'm glad I did it all. I slept with guys all over Manhattan. But, after a while, the experience left me feeling empty. Now, I'm in a committed relationship. And, in comparison, I must say it's even better to have the real thing."

5

New York Dating Challenges

While 63% percent of survey respondents said dating in New York is easier or the same as in other areas, dating in New York does still present its own unique challenges. For many survey respondents, a lack of money equaled a lack of dates. For others, too little time limited their social lives.

I asked New Yorkers, "What are the biggest dating challenges in New York, and how did you overcome those challenges?" And they responded with enthusiasm and words of wisdom. Everyone took a turn being Dear Abby or Ann Landers.

Draven, a 24-year-old gay woman from the suburbs, says "stop looking for people at bars and clubs and start looking somewhere you wouldn't guess, like bookstores," while Camila, a 25-year-old born and raised in New York recommends "keeping three nights a week specifically free for a potential date."

Here are stories of New York dating challenges, and a smattering of good advice to overcome various challenges.

MetroNorth makes me flaccid

"My biggest challenge is living in the suburbs, yet spending my social life in Manhattan. My sex life has suffered. Worrying about the long train ride home (to an area that is kinda scary looking at night) has actually made me flaccid sometimes. I seem to spend so much time just getting from one place to another."—*Jack, a 26-year-old male, originally from Miami*

Money, money, money

"I need a lover that won't drive me crazy. I need a lover that won't want my American Express card. It seems all the women in New York want only two things: credit cards, then divorce lawyers."—*Ace, a 35-year-old male from the suburbs*

"Money, you need money in this town, or the women won't look at you. Damn."—*Raymond, a 41-year-old male, originally from California*

"Money. You have to have lots of expendable cash to date in this town."—*Jocko, a 70-year-old male, originally from Memphis*

"It's expensive to date five women at once!"—NYC Boy, a 36-year-old male, born and raised in New York

"Overpriced apparel, and not enough presidents in your wallet. If you ain't got them, you're not there."—*Aquarius, a 49-year-old female, born and raised in New York*

Money isn't the only thing that matters—cars and fashion are important, too

"To tell you the truth, dating anywhere where commercialism runs wild is tough. On paper, I'm a loser! In reality, there might be more to me than cars, money and f—king stupid fashions."—*Che, a 29-year-old male, born and raised in New York*

The time factor

"It's hard to fit dating into my time schedule. I work a lot and I have other commitments. I am just so busy all the time. I want more than just sex. I want a friend, too. But, that takes time…"—*The Kissing Bandit, a 52-year-old male originally from Boston*

"The challenge is finding the time to get together after you meet someone promising. We're all so busy here, and time is so precious. It's hard to synchronize schedules and find the right evening when neither one of you has a conflict and can actually spend some quality, no-haste time with a new person. For me, I've discovered by keeping three nights a week specifically free for a potential date works best. I let potential dates know this up front, so, they make a great effort to schedule around my schedule."—*Camila, a 25-year-old female, born and raised in New York.*

"There is not enough time in the week to meet all these wonderfully beautiful women in New York!"—*Matthew des Jardins, a 23-year-old male originally from New Mexico.*

"Ugly naked guy" really exists!

"Sometimes I find dating here easy, and other times difficult. Connecting with people that really reveal themselves can be difficult. OK, except for the fat naked guy who lives in the building across from me and shows off his ass while standing in front of the television. He has no problems revealing himself at all."—*NYLivin, a 27-year-old male, originally from Hollywood*

The numbers game

"It's tough to juggle schedules, balance religions and figure out exactly what the other person is looking for. It's a numbers game, just keep dating and dating and dating, and you are bound to find someone."—*Knacka, a 27-year-old male, born and raised in New York*

Bars, meat markets and bookstores

"The biggest challenge is meeting folks. Bars are like meat markets. The streets and the subways rarely work for picking people up. Parties are a great way to meet. The personals are OK, but women don't tend to take men from the personals seriously."—*Norm Penn, a 35-year-old male, born and raised in New York*

"I have a tough time meeting people when I go out. Well, that's not quite true. It's not that hard to talk to people, especially in Brooklyn where I live. But, I'm still not used to giving my number to someone, even after a 20-minute conversation. It still feels like giving my phone number to a complete stranger, and that's just plain scary."—*Alice, a 23-year-old female, originally from North Carolina*

"Biggest challenge is finding someone who's smart, attractive and doesn't just want sex. I think it's hard to find someone who is well rounded. The easiest way I got over that is I stopped looking for people at bars and clubs and looking somewhere you wouldn't guess like bookstores, friends recommendations, concerts. It has actually been great since then."—*Draven, a 24-year-old gay female from the suburbs*

Finding someone—beautiful, yet dumb

"Finding good people. There are lots of beautiful women, but not lots of substance-filled beautiful women." *JimmyJames, a 23-year-old male, originally from New Hampshire*

So many people, so many distractions, so many choices....

"There are so many people here that it can be overwhelming. But, if you just let it flow past, some people stick. You find them."—*NYC-Knows, a 35-year-old female, originally from Houston*

"So many distractions! So many different personalities, and scenes, and expectations. It is tough to get a handle from partner to partner. Each one can be so different from the next. But, that's what make's it exciting, too…"—*Romeo, a 32-year-old male, originally from the mid-Atlantic*

"The biggest dating challenge in NYC is sifting through all the people. To overcome this, I act eccentric and standoffish. I then sleep with the first person who is still willing."—*Blav, a 47-year-old male, originally from upstate New York*

Do I look like a psycho stalker?

"The biggest challenge is trying not to look like a psycho, and then getting the girls comfortable with you." *Gavin, a 25-year-old male, originally from England*

"The challenge is meeting guys I'm attracted to and then getting to actually go out with them (versus having a conversation with them and not getting their phone number.) It's also a challenge to meet guys who aren't psycho, and to help them figure out I'm not psycho either. I've asked out 6 guys in the past three months and they've all said: 'NO.'"—*Micro Bee, a 27-year-old female, originally from San Francisco*

Psycho is okay, just don't be boring

"Biggest challenge is cutting through all the pretense, and the posturing, and all the bullshit, and getting people to level with you. Being on the guest list of the current 'hot' nightspot is of grave importance to a sickening amount of people, and it just gets boring. There may be a lot of psychos in New York, but I think there are a lot more bland, banal types, and in a way, that's worse."—*Tiger, a 26-year-old female, originally from Iowa*

How do I rank on the looks scale?

"I find it challenging to meet girls that are on my level. I do not understand where I fall in terms of looks."—*Mr. Far Side, a 23-year-old male from Long Island*

Culture clash

"One can always find a way to hook up with someone, if you are motivated enough. But, NYC is not the best place for a romantic relationship. Life is too fast and everyone is depressed. It's a bunch of overrated folks wasting time and money. I have a Middle Eastern accent, so instantly, I hit a cultural wall with a lot of folks."—*Toga, a 27-year-old make, originally from Turkey*

Jaded

"Men are guarded here. Professional identity takes precedence over everything else. We are too jaded."—*Rebecca, a 29-year-old female, originally from Boston*

Why people have casual sex

"The biggest challenge is getting past people's boundaries and the walls they put up. They need these walls just to survive here in the city. People are very protective of themselves. But, to break through that barrier and see the real person inside is a hard, daunting and time-consuming task. I think that's why so many people have casual sex. You don't have to deal with really getting to know someone, yet you get the physical attention that all of us need and crave."—*Cowboy, a 22-year-old male from Kansas*

Morons, brats and God's gift

"Women in NYC are so paranoid about everything. There must be a plethora of moron men in this city who ruin it for the nice guys."—*Rico, a 27-year-old male, originally from Dallas*

"The challenge is weeding through the immature brats who think someone died and made them God. One must be patient and just realize the numbers are in your favor in this city."—*Trez, a 36-year-old female from Brooklyn*

"Biggest challenge is the men who think they're God's gift!"—*Elle, a 34-year-old female, born and raised in New York*

The Ivy League clan

"New York is very impersonal. It makes it hard to meet people in a natural way. You have to hustle here. I am a transplant from the Bay Area, so maybe that's why it's harder. I went to school on the west coast and I'm not part of the Ivy League post-college clan that seems to sustain others."—*Jazzman, a 30-year-old male originally from California*

Here! Catch! It's my pick-up line!

"It is hard to get a woman's attention here. They are flying around, doing ten things at once. I think I am going to put my pick-up lines on a card and throw it at them as they run by."—*Niko, a 26-year-old male, originally from San Diego*

Bright lights, big city

"The challenge is to meet decent guys. I overcome this challenge by only dating men that are born and raised in New York, because they don't have the 'bright lights, big city' mentality. For native New Yorkers, this has always been their home, and they know how to treat a lady."—*Cglnyc, a 28-year-old female, originally from Michigan*

A public place

"The two biggest challenges are fear of rejection, and fear of competition. I'm still working on this everyday. It's a part of living here. You sign on to this city, and it's like opening yourself up to the world around you. It's a very public place."—*Brooke, a 29-year-old male, originally from the Bay Area*

I have got to expand my dating circle!

"In order to meet men, go out as much as possible. It's not a good idea to just date friends of friends. I think I need to have people start signing a dating waiver. Having 5 ex-boyfriends at one wedding should be a lesson for everyone to date outside the circle of friends!"—*Tracy, a 30-year-old female, originally from Connecticut*

Dishrags versus ladies

"I've met some very loose women here, and not loose in a good way. At the risk of being crude, the term 'dish rag wh*re' comes to mind. The challenge is distinguishing the ladies from the dish rags."—*Rico, a 23-year-old male, born and raised in New York*

Looking for a core

"I find people here very shallow—maybe it is just more hidden in Europe. I want to find someone with a core, and whom I find physically attractive. I have not yet found this someone."—*Cendrillon, a 29-year-old female, originally from France*

Why don't we get drunk and…

"I like girls who aren't ashamed to go out, get drunk, do drugs, and have a ball. It would seem that this is not socially acceptable here." *LondonMan, a 30-year-old male originally from England*

Workin'…

"The biggest challenge is that work is the only reasonable place to find a mate, but, that sometimes creates its own set of problems. I once quit a job so that I could date a woman from work. She was really impressed with my commitment to going out with her. But, in the end, it didn't work out anyway. But then, I was really glad we didn't work together anymore!"—*Footman, a 41-year-old male, born and raised in New York*

Ah, there's just too much sex. I'm exhausted.

"Deciding to stay home and rest is the biggest hurdle. Any night of the week you can find sex or romance, so just saying 'no' and relaxing at home is really exciting."—*Longhorn, a 33-year-old male, originally from Houston*

"The biggest challenge in New York is holding a relationship together. There is way too much temptation out there. It's so tough to try and be devoted to one person. I've only known my current girlfriend for less than a year and I'm having problems remaining faithful due to all the wonderful temptations out there. So much to tempt me*!"—Lance, a 30-year-old male, originally from Minnesota*

Being single in NYC sucks

"Being single in NYC really sucks. The women I meet are either too young (early 20s) or are very status-oriented. It seems that everyone is already in a relationship, or married. It's hard to get a girl to even call me back! I'm a moderately successful person who is mild-mannered. I guess I have to become more of a jerk or something. A bit of good news, though. Finally, after two years, I've met a down-to-earth person, and we're just starting to date. Wish us luck. It can be so hard to get a relationship to work." *Craig, a 33-year-old male originally from Toronto*

The girls have checklists!

"Girls in New York have checklists. They look for certain specific things and they restrict themselves from dating certain people. The greatest challenge is convincing someone you like, and who likes you, to overcome their predetermined dating requirements and give you a chance."—*BudFox, a 26-year-old male, originally from Boston*

The boys have problems!

"The biggest challenge—meeting a good man. The second biggest challenge—meeting a good man who wants a relationship. I haven't yet overcome this challenge. I turned down a marriage proposal from my then boyfriend in order to pursue my art career. He wanted a family, and I did not. Now, I find myself over 40, and I still don't want a family. I want a companion, and a partner. But, that is just as hard to find. I am looking into younger men, because it seems that all single men over 35 are emotionally dysfunctional."—*Dino, a 41-year-old female, born and raised in New York*

"The challenge is meeting guys that are emotionally available! I have yet to figure out how to overcome this challenge."—*Meg, a 22-year-old female, originally from Boston*

Black and white

"Personally, I find dating in NYC very difficult. I only date white men and I'm black."—*BlackBarbie, a 25-year-old female born and raised in New York*

Dinner together? References, please.

"The biggest challenge to dating in New York is meeting people outside of your immediate circle, or outside of your friends' circles. For the most part, you need to have a good reference just to get a date."—*Henry Paul, a 27-year-old male, originally from upstate New York*

Just don't act like a Long Island guy!

"The biggest challenge of dating in New York is that there are a million other men. You need to be able to stand out. What's the best way to overcome it? I'm not sure. But, I know it's not acting like Long Island guys!"—*Fishbulb, a 28-year-old male, originally from Florida*

Making a connection

"The biggest challenge is the first step—making a connection. When you are on the hunt, it never works. It usually just happens randomly."—*Sam, a 25-year-old gay male, born and raised in New York*

Don't take it too seriously

"The biggest challenge is not to take it all too seriously. It's all about getting to know people and see if it's a fit." *Patrick, a 42-year-old male, born and raised in New York*

There's more to me than my vagina

"The biggest challenge is finding a guy who is not just interested in sex. Finding someone who actually wants a long-term relationship. I have not yet figured out how to overcome this challenge. I've only had one relationship that lasted more than a few months. We dated for about a year, and then out of nowhere, he met a younger woman and dumped me. Another problem I've encountered in New York is that there are so many different cultures, religions, and races living in this city. I've met Jewish guys, and Indian guys, and Puerto Rican guys, etc. who are all perfectly fine sleeping with me, but they would never consider me their girlfriend because I'm not Jewish, or Indian, or Puerto Rican, or whatever. The only way for me to overcome this is to just not even give my number to any guy who is not white, like me. This is disappointing for me, because I really like to get to know people from all cultural backgrounds. But, I also need to be taken seriously by the men I date."—*Starfish, a 26-year-old female*

Sex is not a crime

"This is silly…but I wish having sex was not a criminal act in some situations. Having sex late at night in Central Park, or in a dark alley would be so awesome! But, the risk of being caught is too much to enjoy the event. I mean, come on, there are no little kids running around the Central Park woods at 3 a.m. Why can't the cops let the adults have some thrills? In the meantime, some kid in Queens gets raped and killed because the cops were busy making sure nobody was having sex in the alleys."—*Urban Metaphor, a 22-year-old male from Tennessee.*

Seize the date!

"The biggest challenge is finding someone willing to take a risk. I believe that risks must be taken. If something good comes out of the date, so be it. If not, then you just move on and try again. But, you have to get out there and take the risk!"—*Dee, a 25-year-old female from upstate New York*

Rainbows, peace signs and all that

"What ever happened to the 1969 free love generation? I'm afraid I was born 20 years too late."—*Sky Ace, a 25-year-old male from the suburbs*

Morning. OJ? BJ?

"I've been with the same man for three years now and it's a challenge to keep things fresh and interesting. It's hard to relax at the end of the day, and not be 'bezerk after work.' That's just not conducive to sex. To conquer this challenge? Well, some days I set the alarm half an hour earlier so I can give my man a morning BJ before his OJ. That really helps."—*Jessica, a 28-year-old female, originally from New Hampshire*

Polar

"It's very polar here. There's folks having casual sex, and then there's folks in committed relationship. I don't find much in-between the two."—*New to the City, a 24-year-old female, originally from Baltimore*

The game

"The biggest dating challenge is meeting someone whom you think you could fall for, and then not letting them get too close for fear that you will get hurt. Everyone in this city tries to play the game. Only in the end, the game plays you."—*Kaitlyn, a 23-year-old female, originally from New Jersey*

Honesty—a great tip for a better relationship

"Challenges? There are none for me. I am honest. Honesty gets you a lot further than lying. Most men lie due to insecurities. You'll do much better with women if you just be honest."—*Dust, a 33-year-old male born and raised in New York*

"There are people here that are looking for too much. On the third date, they are already telling you what they see/expect in a mate. You have to be very honest at the start and let them know where you are coming from, so there aren't any mixed signals. "—*Brooklyn, a 31-year-old female from Brooklyn*

"The biggest challenge is finding someone who will be real and honest. New York are known for their candor, but when it comes to getting sex, that trademark honesty takes a beating. I've dated men who've told me everything they thought I wanted to hear, and then once we've had sex, suddenly they mention they are not interested in a relationship. Come on. Just be honest up and upfront. If all you want is sex, so be it. But, don't pretend you want something that you really don't. At least then I'd know where I stood."—*Betty, a 28-year-old female, born and raised in New York*

6

The Battle of the Coasts—Where's it better to be single? New York or California?

In May of 2002, as the research surveys started coming back, I noticed a high percentage of survey respondents were transplants from all over the U.S., and around the world. So, I began asking survey respondents how their New York dating experiences compared to other areas. The exact questions I asked survey respondents were:

> How would you rate dating in New York compared to other areas?
> How would you rate your sexual experiences in New York versus other areas?
> Any other comments regarding the dating scene in New York?

As these responses started coming back, I noticed many folks contrasting sex/dating on the East Coast versus the West Coast. So, I added one final question:

> For those of you who've lived, dated or had sex on both coasts, how does sex on the East Coast compare to the West Coast? Please be specific in your comparisons.

The responses were marvelous! Spicy, confrontational, conflicting, and everything you'd hope for when writing a saucy book such as this.

Now, the East Coast vs. West Coast question was not added until June of 2002, so not all survey respondents had a chance to answer this question. To gather more responses on this juicy topic, I posted notes on two online bulletin boards, craigslist Bay area, (**http://www.craigslist.org/**) and craigslist New York, **http://newyork.craigslist.org/** asking the singles on both Coasts to sound off. Now, when talking about dating on the East Coast versus the West Coast, one could have just as easily included Los Angeles, Seattle, Boston, etc. Since my editorial deadline was fast bearing down on me, I focused on San Francisco and New York City, with a couple of L.A. jabs thrown in. Want to sound off on your favorite East Coast or West Coast city? Please email your comments to **kianatower@aol.com** and I'll post them on **www.sexinsiliconvalley.com**. The Battle of the Coasts will rage on!

Without further ado, here are the results of the first battle of the Coasts!

Folks on the West Coast Defend Their Dating Turf

West Coast—more fun to be queer!

"It's just more fun to be queer in San Francisco, than it is to be queer in New York. The NYC queer community is tame. The San Francisco dykes are into exciting things like S&M, and non-monogamy. In New York, the dykes want to either keep it quiet, or pretend they're not all that kinky. Come on! Let's spice it up a little, like they do on the West Coast!"—*Brooklyn Red, a 29 year old gay female, born and raised in New York.*

West Coast is friendlier!

"The East Coast dating scene is not as friendly as the West Coast. NYC people have a 'rush' attitude. The NYC men are sneaky, sly, and somewhat cocky. Even though I live in New York, I prefer dating women who are originally from other parts of the country. They're just friendlier."—*Nice Guy, a 40 year old male, born and raised in New York*

Mellow out, baby!

"New York is faster paced than California. People in New York tend to be more aggressive than the West Coasters. Californians are just mellower folks."—*Danny, a 32 year old male, originally from California*

The Princesses from Long Island and New Jersey

"In NYC, you have old established wealth and the princesses from Long Island and Jersey. It's all about who you know. When I lived in New York, I became friends with some fashion models. It was amazing how much 'cooler' strangers thought I was, even though I was the same person. The San Francisco dating scene is friendlier. People won't tell you to 'f--k off' like they do in New York City, although I must admit, sometimes I miss that forthright honesty."—*Joe, a 31 year old male from San Francisco*

Mixed review

"I've lived in Los Angeles, then New York, then San Francisco. First, on the side of New York, there is more diversity in the people on the East Coast. The women there are so wonderfully complex! Here in San Francisco, it's a 'one company' town. Everyone talks about technology, in one form or another. It gets dull. However, on the side of California, we have incredible variety in the types of activities offered. In the same weekend, you'll be encouraged to check out things like the World Cup Final party in Kezar stadium at 4 a.m., and then also be encouraged to check out the fun happenings at the Gay Pride Fair. And, Californians have much more relaxed attitudes than New Yorkers."—*Matt, a 31-year-old male, lives in San Francisco*

Bohemian!

"A couple of differences between East and West. The vibe here on the West Coast is bohemian. Plus, West Coasters tend to be more touchy-feeling than NYC. Then, there's the intensity of New Yorkers. In New York, if you approach someone on the street to ask something, they will keep walking. It's not because they don't want to help, but rather you should keep up with them and walk along. In San Francisco, people are more inclined to stop."—*Mike, a 29-year-old male from San Francisco*

Dating Advice

I sent follow-up questions to a couple of the interviewees and asked what dating advice they would give to someone new to the West Coast dating scene. Here are the responses…

"New to the San Francisco singles scene? Well, be aware that 40 % of the men are gay. And if you're a 6'3", blue-eyed professional male living in Pacific Heights as I am, it's a wonderful, wonderful thing. I feel like a kid in a candy store."—*Felix, a 32-year-old gay male from San Francisco*

"A woman that should know once told me this, '33% are gay, 33% are married, 33% are assholes in SF.'" *James, a 34 year old male from San Francisco*

"It is soooo different out here on the West Coast. I'm from the East Coast, born in New Jersey and spent a few years in Manhattan before moving West. I have been here for five years and I still haven't figured it all out. But here are some thoughts: People here are far more 'scared.' It seems people will not go for the chance encounter like many do back East. Women seem to be aloof, and the men aren't assertive enough. Most people out here seem to meet and hook up with people from work, something I didn't do back East."—*Michael, a 40-year-old male from San Francisco.*

"The Bay Area dating scene is deceptively simple: All of the women are in SF, but all of the men are in Silicon Valley (50 miles south, in case you didn't know). Like migratory birds, the Valley Men flock to the city each weekend in search of attention, sex, love, companionship, and all of the fabulous things that a good woman can provide. For the Valley Man, this struggle between his professional drive and his desire to procreate is the central theme of his life. What's a San Fran girl to do? Visit the Valley and try smoking the birds out of their caves."—*Johnny, a 38-year-old male from San Francisco.*

Why the East Won the Day

In the battle of the Coasts, the New Yorkers grew very passionate in defending their city. They felt that the best sex, by far, is to be had on the right coast. Want to sound off on East Coast sex versus West Coast sex? Email **KianaTower@aol.com**. Time to defend the sexual rep of your Coast!

L.A. is an endless, mindless sprawl. New York has a cozy, intimate scale.

"Dating on the East Coast versus the West Coast? I lived in L.A. for a year, and spent the rest of my life in New York. L.A. was too car-centric for me. Here in New York, I just love to walk—looking at people and things, shopping around, looking at the street nightlife, and the hip restaurants. New York has a cozy intimate scale, compared to the endless, mindless sprawl that is LA."—*Kevin, a 33-year-old male, born and raised in New York*

East Coast people are more real

"I think people in New York are more real. There is less bullshit. I also think it is less about looks on the East Coast. West Coast folks are so caught up in the looks thing." *Roxy, a 33-year-old female from New Jersey*

West Coast men more interested in computers than sex?

"During the rise of the Internet boom, men in California just were not interested in sex. All they did was work. All work and no sex makes California men very dull boys."—*Little Fifi, a 28-year-old gay male, originally from upstate New York*

West Coast men not as sexy?

"I lived in San Diego for a while, and found it very easy to meet guys that were good looking, but the men were just not as sexy as the men in New York."—*Michael B., a 33-year-old gay male, born and raised in New York*

Prefer to date women from the East Coast

"San Francisco is a tough 'singles city.' For some reason, everyone is just either busy or taken. I prefer to date people from the East Coast."—Jason, a 29-year-old male from San Francisco.

Tough to get to know Californians

"I think Californians are tougher to get to know than New Yorkers. People have said it's a lot more work. People tend to keep to themselves, and you had to do more work to meet someone."—*Zach, a 37-year-old male from San Francisco*

It's just so easy to meet people in New York!

"New York is a great place to date. There are many more single women than men. There's lots of 'friction,' e.g. I've picked up women on the train, at bus stops, sharing cabs, etc."—*NYC Boy, a 36-year-old male born and raised in New York*

"This is one of the best places on earth to date. From my experience, it has been so easy! There are so many single women. This is the only place I've ever been where you can have a date with a different girl every night. I don't know how I will ever settle down."—*Matthew des Jardins, a 23 year old male originally from New Mexico*

"NYC is a great place to date. You'll always meet a mixed crowd. You can go anywhere, and meet just about any type of person."—*Potion, a 21-year-old female born and raised in New York*

Moaning! Groaning! Hello, neighbor!

"Sex in New York is better than other areas I've been. The abundance of people all around makes having sex at home feel like sex in public. When I open the bedroom window, the neighbors cheer when my girlfriend moans out loud. It's exciting."—*Urban Metaphor, a 22-year-old New Yorker*

Swinging from lampshades

"People in New York are more sexually conservative than you would otherwise expect. Maybe it's because there is so much to do here that folks never get bored enough, whereas in Peoria, you're more willing to swing from lampshades and such." *Footman, a 41-year-old male born and raised in New York*

What a timesaver!

"I've had amazing experiences here. OK, I've had amazing experiences everywhere, but the experiences I've had in NYC would have taken a lot longer to find in other places."—*Dylan, a 23 year old male, originally from the Midwest*

OK, you two managed to shock Kiana Tower with this one!

"The librarians here in New York have a surprisingly high sex drive. Their libidos need caressing after sitting around all day!"—*Sky Ace, a 35-year-old male from the suburbs*

"Never underestimate the power of a female librarian. She could have a lot of built-up sexual tension that needs to be slowly relieved. I find a lot of foreplay at some various times in the New York Public Library. Ex Librus."—*Alan, male, born and raised in New York*

Beautiful and sassy

"All the men and women in NYC happen to be tremendously beautiful. They come in all shapes and sizes and in every flavor that waters your taste buds. We are opinionated, straightforward, and have that sassy NYC attitude that makes this the greatest city in the world."—*Dean, a 25 year old male from New York.*

New Yorkers offer dating advice

So, to keep the challenge fair, I asked New Yorkers what advice they would dole out to a girl that was new in town, and looking to find herself a nice man. Here's their advice:

"New York City has different singles scenes—from bar/lounges, clubs to the gym, cafes & even Central Park (Sheep Meadow for instance.)

You can meet new faces, without the attitude, at Gallery openings, gyms, and the dog walk. Also, participate in the activities you love the most. You will find someone who likes doing the same thing."—*Eddy, a 28-year-old male from New York*

"East versus West? New York's dating scene is much the same, but things seem to move at a faster pace than L.A. On both coasts, beware folks who are superficial. If you're a genuine person who really want a nice relationship void of games, disappointment and heartache, do yourself a favor—don't just look for a pretty face. Make an effort to meet people with whom you'll have a common ground activity, such as a dance lesson, or even working for the same firm, (although it best be a very, very large firm, to be safe.) This is a much better approach than the bar scene. In New York, you're either into having a serious relationship or you're part of the 90% who are playing the field. You have to ask yourself, which are you?"—*Jason, a 35-year-old male from New York*

"East versus West? I'm from the Bay area, so I can offer up a good comparison. Dating in New York is very different.

If you're a woman, you need to know about the Hampton Type—the jock from high school who never grew up. He'll have college stories, or high school stories, that get retold over and over against the backdrop of the Hamptons in the summer, or the latest trendy bar in the winter.

Then, there are the millionaires, or those that want to be. Yeah, NYC is filled with them. There's nothing special about them, other than they have a bit of money. The food is better, but that's about it. You have to make up for the lack of company.

That leaves a small population of men to date in NYC. They are volunteers and hard workers. They can be found in bookstores, at work, at the park, and in the grocery store, and occasionally they can be disguised as the Hampton type, or the millionaire type. When you do find one you'd like to date, treat him with kindness and consider yourself lucky. Don't be stupid and drop him for the first pretty boy to walk your way, because that pretty boy is going to turn out to be gay, and then what are you going to do?

If you're a man, good luck to you. The women can be difficult, OK, borderline impossible. If you try to meet someone at a bar or club, you're most likely going to get stuck with someone with a lot of attitude, who can't talk about anything other than shopping. If you're looking for someone who is fun and outgoing, easy-going and down-to-earth, then you'll need to do a little work. Consider volunteer work. Nycares has a website of stuff to do around the city. Keep your chin up. You can meet a nice woman.

As for the major faux pas, here are the rules:

1. if you ask her out, you pay

2. open doors—we women like that

3. be nice at all times

4. breathe

5. don't knock romance, it works

6. get to know her before jumping into bed

7. if she sleeps with you on the first date, you're not the first or last one she'll be doing that with

Good luck."—*Gloria, age unknown, originally from California*

About the Author

I was born in 1969 in Sleepy Hollow, New York. As a child, I loved writing and telling stories. By age 4, my Mom decided: "This one's going to be a writer one day!" Mom was right.

I graduated college in 1991 with degrees in English and Communications. One of my favorite college activities was being a DJ at my college's hip little FM rock station. My radio station experience, and my "radio voice," proved very handy for doing radio interviews for my first book. Recently, I was in the midst of a radio interview, relaying a story from book, when the host of the radio show declared: "What a voice! You should consider doing radio!"

After college, I landed an exciting (albeit very low-paying) job in the creative department of a Manhattan advertising agency. This job led to a position at a small TV station in Manhattan, which then led to a job in the Public Relations department of a high-tech company. I found that I loved working in high-tech, and by 1996, I decided Silicon Valley was the place to be. So I left my job in New York, packed up all my possessions into a clumsy, worn-out U-Haul, and drove 3,000 miles to California, with my faithful dog Max as my traveling companion.

I fell in love with California. And…fell in love. My career path here was bumpy at times, with my first two employers going belly-up. But the third company went straight to IPO heaven, and left me with the funds to live in a cozy beach house, where I still live today.

One chilly Sunday morning in Santa Cruz, I was surfing (in the water, not on the Internet) when…it happened. The most handsome man I'd ever seen paddled out, said hello and proceeded to carve through the morning waves like a Hawaiian surf god. I watched him, mesmerized, and fell more in love with every wave.

I married that man.

Not only was he profoundly sexy, he was a brilliant high-tech engineer with an outstanding career record in Silicon Valley. I had found myself a "supergeek." The ultimate man—body, brains, and personality.

A few months later, I was out to dinner with a group of friends in Silicon Valley. The topic turned to sex.

Everyone had a story to tell, and a desire to tell it. The stories were outrageous, funny, sad, and downright fascinating. I decided it was the perfect subject material for a book. That night, with the encouragement of my friends, I began writing the stories down, and creating the rough framework for what became "Sex in Silicon Valley."

Eager for more material to fill the book, I recruited a friend to partner with me on the project, and we created www.sexinsiliconvalley.com. We posted notes on Bay Area electronic bulletin boards, asking singles to spill the dirt on their dating lives. The site was an immediate hit, generating thousands of hits in its first week alone. We received a huge wealth of data, and compiled the best of the stories into the final book "Sex in Silicon Valley—the geeks in the Valley are getting more than you'd think."

There was only one problem. Some of the stories were very explicit, and my writing partner and I worked at respected high-tech companies. So, we created "Kiana Tower." I would act as the voice and the face of Kiana Tower, and my friend would be my silent partner.

How did the book do? Not bad, all in all. In just six weeks, the book rose to the top 3% of all books sold on Amazon.com. The book attracted the attention of radio and TV producers, and I was interviewed over 40 times on stations throughout the country. Did the book become a bestseller? (cough, cough) Um…no. Not yet, anyway. But, I very much enjoyed the process of creating and promoting the book. (Yes, even those 3 AM radio interviews. Sleep? Who needs sleep?) I enjoyed the whole process so much that I began working on this sequel—"100 Happy Naked New Yorkers." I hope you enjoy reading my books, as much as I enjoy writing them. Please feel free to contact me with your feedback, both positive and negative, at **kianatower@aol.com**. Constructive criticism, and glowing words of praise, are equally welcomed.

APPENDIX A

The Survey Questions

To gather the research for the book, I created an online survey and posted it on **www.sexinsiliconvalley.com**. I contacted New York singles through Internet bulletin boards, such as craigslist, Yahoo! New York and Salon.com's personals. I invited the singles to sound off with their opinions. The exact survey is forwarded in its entirety below.

Interested in sharing your own dating stories? I am gathering research data for a future book which will encompass stories of singles from all over the United States. Please feel free to submit your stories, thoughts and opinions at **www.sexinsiliconvalley.com**.

New York Survey

To protect your privacy, you will be referred to by a pen name.

Choose a pen name:

Please keep it clean. We reserve the right to modify pen names as necessary

How did you hear about this survey?

Age:

Gender:

☐ Male

☐ Female

Do you live in:

☐ New York City

☐ Suburbs

☐ Upstate New York

☐ Tri-state area

☐ Other (please specify) [   ]

Are you originally from New York?

☐ Yes, I am a native.

☐ No, I am a transplant.

If you are a transplant, where are you from?

[   ]

What brought you to New York?

[   ]

How long have you lived in New York?

[   ]

Occupation:

[   ]

Are you:

- ☐ Single
- ☐ Married or Same-Sex Union
- ☐ Separated
- ☐ Divorced
- ☐ Other (*please specify*)

In general, how would you rate dating in New York compared to other areas?

- ☐ More difficult to get dates
- ☐ Easier to get dates
- ☐ About the same as other areas
- ☐ Have not lived in other areas

Comments:

In general, how would you rate your sexual experiences in New York compared to other areas?

- ☐ Better
- ☐ Worse
- ☐ About the same as other areas
- ☐ Have not lived in other areas

Comments:

For those of you who've lived, dated or had sex on both coasts, how does sex on the East Coast compare to the West Coast? Please be specific in your comparisons.

How have the events of 9/11 affected your romantic/sex life?

Would you like to make any other comments regarding 9/11, or sex in New York in general?

What's the most unusual place in New York you have ever had sex? Tell us the details...

Describe you biggest dating disaster in New York.

What are the biggest dating challenges in New York? How did you overcome those challenges?

By clicking "Submit" you agree to grant Kiana Tower unrestricted rights to publish the above in print and online.

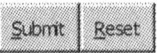

APPENDIX B

The Survey Results

Age:
Average: 32.6 years

Gender:
Male: 63%
Female: 37%

Occupation:
Administrative: 4%
Architect: 1%
Craftsman: 1%
Editor/Writer/Journalist/Works in Publishing: 11%
Executive: 2%
Finance: 11%
Film/TV: 4%
Freelance: 2%
Hair Stylist: 1%
Insurance: 1%
Legal: 4%
Model/Fashion Industry: 2%
Music Industry: 5%
Non-Profit: 1%
Project Manager: 1%
Retired: 2%
Sales/Marketing: 7%
'Slacker': 1%

Student: 7%
Tech: 11%
Unemployed: 3%
Various other, or no occupation listed: 18%

Do you live in:
New York City: 82%
Suburbs: 7%
Upstate New York: 3%
Tri-state Area: 5%
Others: 3%

Are you originally from New York?
Natives: 40%
Transplants: 60%

If you are a transplant, what brought you to New York?
'A boy'/'A girl': 8%
Aspiring writer: 4%
The Arts: 12%
Bright Lights/Big City: 2%
College/Graduate School: 14%
Desire to experience freedom: 4%
'Fame and fortune': 1%
Family: 8%
Friends: 2%
'Life': 1%
'Hated Atlanta': 1%
Nightclubs: 1%
'Tired of California:' 1%
'To get away from Atlanta': 1%
'To get the hell out of Florida': 1%
'To get out of Kansas:' 1%
'To get out of the mid-West: 1%

Weather: 1%
"'Woody Allen's movie: *Manhattan*': 1%
Work/Career: 32%

Are you:
Single: 81%
Married or Same-Sex Union: 10%
Separated/Divorced: 9%

In general, how would you rate dating in New York compared to other areas?
More difficult to get dates: 37%
Easier to get dates: 48%
About the same as other areas: 15%

In general, how would you rate your sexual experiences in New York compared to other areas?
Better: 44%
Worse: 15%
 About the same as other areas: 32%

Sexual orientation:
Gay: 8%
Hetero: 92%

How have the events of 9/11 affected your romance/sex life?
Negative impact: 14%
Scene changed for the better: 32%
Little or no change: 54%

Appendix C

A preview of my next novel: Life Stories

By Kiana Tower

Introduction: For as long as I've been able to write, I've always written short stories. As an imaginative child, I wrote fanciful stories on any numbers of topics, and even completed a science fiction novel for a young writers' contest. (I didn't win.) But, as I grew and matured, I discovered my greatest strength was simply writing about life. I began to write about moments in my life that "stuck in my gut." Once I started sharing writings about significant life moments, I noticed my writings now elicited emotional reactions out of readers. I realized then that non-fiction was my forte. (I have a hunch my fictional writings weren't all that good anyway, much as my parents politely fussed over them.)

Last weekend, I experienced one of those gut-sticking moments. It happened on the highway near my house, and I couldn't get the experience out of my head until I wrote it down. I call this story "The Old Man on the Highway" and it is the first in a collection called "Life Stories," which will be published in the summer of 2003.

The Old Man on the Highway
—an excerpt from the upcoming book "Life Stories"

It was an overcast Saturday morning. My husband, Joe, and I were headed to "the city" to run errands. We live in a sleepy fishing village, and periodically need to journey down the Pacific Coast Highway to reach a small city with more shops available. As we headed south along the highway, we saw an old man walking along the opposite side of the road, slowly heading north. He had a little blue knapsack on his back, and he was hunched over with age.

"He'll never get very far at that pace!" I joked, assuming the old man was just a wayward tourist from one of the many state parks that dot the region.

We ran our errands, and two hours later we were headed home, north on the highway.

We saw the same old man, now several miles down the road, still making his way slowly and steadily.

"Wow, he's walked a long way," I commented. I also noticed he was now nowhere near any of the state parks. But there he was, still walking.

I got a sinking feeling in my stomach as I realized he wasn't a tourist, out for a healthy stroll. He was a homeless man, making his way on a very long stretch of highway.

Still, we kept driving, and headed home to get on with our Saturday. We did the things that couples do on Saturdays, tidying up the house, gardening, lovemaking while the baby naps. Several hours later, I headed out again, this time to take our dogs for a hike on a seaside cliff trail. As I turned my truck onto the highway, there he was. The same old man. Still making his way steadily northward.

I kept driving.

I spent a pleasant late afternoon clambering along the seaside trail with the happy, sniffing, urinating dogs. We hiked until the evening fog blustered in off the water with an icy chill. I whistled for the dogs, and headed for the truck, looking forward to a hot dinner at home.

As I pulled the truck back onto the highway, the tired dogs already snoring in the cab, I passed the same old man. Now, even further down the highway. Still moving at the same slow, steady pace.

I kept driving.

When I arrived home, my husband Joe, and our six month old son were asleep in the rocking chair. I started making dinner, my mind filled with images of the old man, walking steadily along.

"Hey," Joe said, opening one sleepy eye, and watching me move about the kitchen.

I laid the uncooked chicken onto a platter and started to season it.

"That old man was still walking," I said, sprinkling on a generous amount of seasoned salt.

"Yeah? Where was he?" asked my husband, sitting up with interest.

I described his last location.

"We should help him," Joe said. He eyed the platter of chicken. "He needs that chicken more than we do."

"Yes!" I was thrilled. I hadn't even voiced the thought that was in my head, yet my husband had just spoken the words aloud.

"Hurry up and cook the chicken," Joe said, looking out the window at the thickening evening fog, "it's getting dark, and we won't be able to find him in the dark."

I stood anxiously over the grill, willing the chicken to cook faster, as the sun struggled to set through the thickening fog. The lights of the setting sun danced unevenly over the ocean, competing in shades of light and dark with the moving, living fog. My mind started going over all the places a homeless man might decide to spend the night. Would we find him before he tucked himself safely away in a crevice to sleep?

"Pack him some bananas, and oranges, and bottled water, too," Joe advised, when I came in for a break, to get away from the smoky grill.

I quickly raided the pantry, filling a bag with the oranges, the bananas, the water, and then throwing in a bag of soy nuts and a plastic tub full of cereal for good measure.

I looked over at Joe and our infant son. The lights of the television news danced off their faces.

"Ah, the California lottery," Joe said, digging into his wallet for the ticket he'd purchased earlier that day.

"Nope, not a winner," Joe said a few moments later. He crumpled up the ticket.

I went back outside to tend the chicken.

"Come on chicken, cook!" I urged the clueless meat, watching nightfall encroach upon the patio with the suddenness it always does when you wish for daylight.

Finally, the chicken was done. The meat peeled back nicely from the bone, the skin was crispy and speckled with seasoning. I brought the chicken in, wrapped it carefully in foil before adding it to the bag of food.

"Let's go," Joe said, quickly strapping our son into his carseat.

We hurried down the stairs, looking out the window as the last rays of the sun faded away.

"I hope we're not too late," I said.

I grabbed the binoculars on the way out. Joe gave me a questioning look.

"If I were homeless, I'd bunk down at the beach," I told Joe, "maybe we can spot him from the cliff."

We piled into the truck, and pulled away from the house. Joe asked me to describe in detail where I'd seen him last.

"He was on Main Street, by the gas station, still heading north."

Joe drove slowly up Main Street, while I carefully scanned both sides of the street, paying attention to doorways, and other crevices where he might be bunked down for the night.

No sign of him.

We kept driving.

"Could he have gotten this far?" Joe wondered out loud.

In the back seat, the baby started howling, restless to be out of his seat. Neither Joe nor I wanted to give up but now we had a howling infant, demanding attention.

I looked and looked, hoping to catch some glimpse of the man. The bag of food was warm in my hands, the heat of the fresh cooked chicken emanating out. The car smelled delicious from the fresh bar-beque, and my stomach growled, reminding me we hadn't eaten. The baby's cries grew louder and more insistent, and more grating on the nerves.

But, still we looked.

"Please God," I prayed silently, "help us find this man so we can help him."

"There he is!" shouted Joe. Joe pointed, and took the turn off from Main Street to the highway.

And there he was. Still walking steadily on, with that little blue knapsack on his back. On the highway. Heading north.

We pulled over, and the man approached the car.

"Lock the doors as soon as I get out," I instructed Joe, "we don't want him getting in the car."

Now that we found him, I suddenly realized the man could be dangerous—perhaps mentally ill or drugged out or drunk. We didn't want him climbing in the backseat next to the baby, thinking we were offering him a ride. I knew I could defend myself enough to get back into the car, but I didn't want to take any chances with the baby. I did a quick mental review of all the self-defense classes I'd taken—eye jabs, nose bashes, knee to the groin, etc.

I climbed out of the car and approached the man with the bag of food. Behind me, I heard Joe click the automatic locks. They were safely locked in. I was safely locked out. I was a little scared, not knowing what to expect.

The man walked slowly up to me, and looked into my face. His eyes were clear. There were no cloudings in his eyes from drugs or alcohol.

His face was tanned from the sun. His blue eyes pierced into mine. His skin was wrinkled, and deeply tanned from a life spent outdoors. He reminded me of a wise old wizard.

"We saw you walking," I started.

He nodded slowly, reminding me of an old sage.

"Um, there's food and water, and nuts, and fruit, and chicken. We just barbequed it. It's still hot," I said, peering into the bag, before handing it over.

"Thank you," he said, in a voice deep and sincere.

There was nothing more to say. I nodded, and got back into the car.

We drove away, heading up the highway a bit until we could turn around, and then heading back toward him. As we passed the old man, Joe and I craned our necks to get a good look at the old man. He was carefully unpacking the food we'd given him, and repacking it into his little blue knapsack. Before we drove out of eyeshot, I saw him open the foil wrapped package containing the chicken, and take a deep whiff.

I smiled over at Joe.

Joe grabbed my hand and gave it a squeeze. He looked at me, with a smile that stretched all the way to his eyes, "We just won the lottery, know that?"

That night, as we lay comfortably in bed, our bellies full from sandwiches and fruit, we reflected on our lives. We spoke in soft voices, so as not to awaken our quietly slumbering son. We spoke of everything we had to be grateful for. We both have good jobs, in a time when many are out of work. We have a son, when there are many not able to have children. We have a house, in a time when many are homeless. We have a fridge full of food, when many are going hungry. We fell asleep feeling very content, and very blessed. The old man had indeed given us a precious gift.

And, the old man is still out there. Walking slowly northward.

Appendix D

An excerpt from: "Sex in Silicon Valley—the geeks of the Valley are getting more than you'd think"

Early in 2002, I published my first book *Sex in Silicon Valley—the geeks of the Valley are getting more than you'd think*. The book was an intimate peek into the Silicon Valley social scene, with Bay area residents sharing true stories about dating, relationships and sex.

New Yorkers responded very favorably to the book, and proved to be my biggest market. As a thank you to the people of New York, I wanted to end this book with a big freebie. Forwarded below, you will find an entire collection of stories from *Sex in Silicon Valley*. I picked a couple of the most popular stories from every chapter in the book, and included them below.

Now, a word of warning. *Sex in Silicon Valley* is a much more…ah, 'detailed' book than *100 Happy Naked New Yorkers*. These stories include more graphic descriptions of singles doing the wild things that singles do. So, if talk of penises is offensive to you, I'd recommend skipping this chapter. If, however, you enjoy a good yarn about human beings getting it on, then you'll find these tales most entertaining.

If you'd like to more tales such as these, and see the stories I deemed much too hot to include in the excerpt below, I encourage you to check out the full text of *Sex in Silicon Valley*, available from Amazon.com.

Enjoy!

◆   ◆   ◆

an excerpt from the chapter:
"Why write about sex in Silicon Valley?"

Imagine this…

You're out with friends somewhere in the Bay Area. The wine and banter are flowing freely. As you drink and laugh, the conversation turns to sex. Everyone has a story to tell, and the more stories people tell, the more the laughter flows.

"Okay, Okay…what's the most unusual place you've ever had sex?" you ask your friends. "Your ideal sexual encounter?" "Your worst dating disaster?" All sorts of funny and memorable stories come up. This book is about those stories.

Some come on in, pull up a chair, have a drink, and read on…

A Word About Silicon Valley

Statistics show Bay Area denizens read more books, have more years of schooling, and as we go to press, have the highest per capita income in the nation. This affluent, literate, highly educated populace seems to have everything going for it. Up until the recent dot com bust, tales of newly-minted millionaires and optionaires paying cash for houses and cars dominated the media. Silicon Valley became the place financial dreams came true for anyone smart enough, and lucky enough, to hit a pot of stock option gold.

But, along with the reputation for free flowing wealth came a stereotype of a Silicon Valley geek who led a terribly dull life, consisting only of endless hours in a cubicle. No social life. And certainly, no sex,

This book, written during the times of both the dot com boom and the dot com busts of 2000 and 2001, sets out to shatter the geek stereotype. While admittedly, those of us who live here in the Valley do work insane hours in dull carpeted cubicles, we do have social lives, and we do have sex, For some of our interviewees, their sex lives didn't even begin to get interesting until they moved to the Bay area.

"Sex in Silicon Valley" combines stories and research from 300 Silicon Valley residents, ranging in age from 21 to 56, and working in professions ranging from graphic design to rocket research. This book includes a large assortment of great stories of what we're really doing here when we're not ensconced in our cubicles…or when we are in our cubicles (and no one's around).

Researching Sex in Silicon Valley

But, more than just great stories, the authors of this book were interested in gathering statistical data on the Silicon Valley dating scene. (Hey, what kind of geeks would we be if we didn't gather data?) The dating scene here fascinated us, and not just because we live and date here ourselves. Silicon Valley is filled with such a diverse population of people—an extraordinarily bright collection of tech-oriented folks from every corner of the globe. Even in today's tough economic times, the Valley is still instilled with a spirit of innovation—the feeling that with enough hard work and combined brain power, anything is possible. This is a fascinating place to live and work.

As we began conducting research and gathering data, the results of a much-publicized 1999 Census Bureau survey caught our eye. The survey gave Silicon Valley the dubious distinction of having the largest single-man surplus of any major metropolitan area in the country, surpassing even the traditional man-surplus capital, Anchorage, Alaska.

We designed an extensive web survey, polling Silicon Valley and Bay Area residents about dating, relationships and their social lives. We got the word out using popular bulletin boards, such as craigslist (www.craigslist.org). Within hours of its launch, our survey site had attracted more than a thousand hits!

In addition, we conducted in-person interviews with colleagues, friends and everyone we knew, with a promise of complete anonymity. Over various dinners and get-togethers of margaritas, sushi and pizza, we continued to ask questions and gather data. After months of careful research, we had more than 300 usable surveys and first-person interviews. Our research was complete. And, we discovered, there truly is Sex in Silicon Valley!

an excerpt from the chapter:
Dating in Silicon Valley: The Good, the Bad and the Ugly

The Good

Survey respondents had wildly mixed opinions on the challenges of dating in the Bay Area. Almost half—47 percent—of survey respondents from out of the area reported that dating in Silicon Valley was more challenging than in other areas, while only 25 percent said it was easier. But the majority of those surveyed claimed the quality of sexual encounters (60 percent) and sex partners (56 percent) was better in the Valley.

Many reported frustrations that tied right into a 1999 Census Bureau survey which found that Silicon Valley had the largest single-man surplus of any major metropolitan area in the country. According to the census bureau, Silicon Valley's lopsided dating ratio surpasses even the traditional man-surplus capital, Anchorage, Alaska. As one respondent put it, "Silicon Valley is a single woman's dating paradise."

Our survey results mirrored the inequality of the sexes; 61 percent of respondents were male, 39 percent female. And while we did receive a fair amount of responses from frustrated men, hundreds of the survey respondents who shared their stories on SexinSiliconValley.com showed another side of the Valley—the wonderful spirit of innovation that made this Valley great is now being applied to the challenges of dating.

Many survey respondents, male and female, straight and gay, reported ample opportunities for sex and dating in Silicon Valley. Some even went so far as to describe the sexual opportunities here as "the best they've ever had." As one respondent said, "There are so many intelligent, creative 'engineer' types who apply the same type of inventiveness to sex. There are amazing men sitting behind computers thinking about sex all day—hot and ready to go! Ditto for women."

Here are a few of their stories.

Jon

Jon is a 32 year-old Lab Technician, originally from Mission Viejo, California. Jon gives the Silicon Valley dating scene high marks. He ranks dating here as easier than other areas, opportunities for sex as more readily available, and the quality of sex partners as better than other areas.

"There are lot of like-minded people in this area," says Jon. "It makes it much easier to find dates."

Compared to other areas, Jon finds people in the Bay Area more straight forward. "There is a less pretext here," says Jon. "People know what they want. This area is conducive to instant gratification, whether it's sexual or otherwise."

Jon is a big fan of cybersex. "It is easy, cheap and fun—the ultimate safe sex experience!"

Jon enjoys sex over 10 times a month with his significant other, and ranks his last sexual encounter as an eight out of 10. "It was really hot," says Jon. "Everything was done by non-verbal communication. No words were necessary. Just lots of eye contact and knowing just how to please each other. I felt really connected with her!"

When asked about his best sex ever, Jon remembers his earliest sexual experiences. "The best ever was the second time I had sex. The first time was rushed, and I just wanted to get it over with so I could get past being a virgin. The second time was so different—so fluid and beautiful. I was with my girlfriend in a small cabin in Carmel. I didn't even know we were going to do it—which was part of what made it so cool! We went from one phase to another, and I felt like we literally melted together."

When asked if he had any other comments, Jon says: "Shhhhhh! I'll let you in on a little secret. I like to have cybersex as a woman. I go into lesbian chat rooms, and get women off, posing as a woman myself. It's awesome!"

Mamie

Mamie is a 25 year-old Administrative Assistant from Kansas. When asked why she came to the Bay Area, Mamie answered: "Bright Lights, Big City."

Mamie has been in the Bay Area for three years, and is currently single. She finds dating here easier than in her native Kansas. She also finds the sexual partners to be of better quality.

The last time she had sex was "with a co-worker. What was good about it? Well, it wasn't weird afterwards at work. Not for long, anyway. Just casual. No strings attached. You couldn't do that in

When comparing the Bay Area to other areas she has lived, Mamie comments: "I've lived in Kansas and in Atlanta, and sex there is something you only talk about in whispers and do in the dark. Here, sex is not such a taboo subject. You can talk about it, and about getting it, without seeming scared of it. It seems more fun, without worrying about being labeled as being slutty.

There are other advantages to being single here. People stay single here longer than in other parts of the country. No one expects a 30 year-old single person to not have ever played around.

In Kansas, if you are 30 and have never been married, you would be considered an old maid who is over the hill, and kind of pathetic. Not here. 30 year-olds are considered as being in their prime here."

For some women, Silicon Valley is truly a single woman's dating paradise. They find the quality and availability of sexual partners to be superior to other areas, with more than enough opportunities to keep a single woman very happy and occupied. Here are the stories of ladies who are enjoying stellar sex in the Bay Area…

Joy

Joy is a 34 year-old Finance Director, originally from Arizona. Joy came to Silicon Valley seven years ago for a job. She is unmarried, but currently in a committed relationship.

She finds dating in Silicon Valley easier than other areas. "People are more friendly and approachable here," says Joy. "Mostly the common demographics makes it possible—majority of people I come into contact with are 25-40, professional, college-degreed, etc."

She finds the quality, and availability of sexual partners to be better than other areas. "More men than woman, do the math! Being single, female, fairly attractive, fit… Hey, it's way too easy to get laid here."

Joy also enjoys the sensitive sides of the men she has met here. "Men here are more fragile, open up emotionally easier, and you can connect with them better. It takes a soft voice and a soft touch to completely melt away any feigned machismo or toughness in just a few minutes… more intelligent people also seem to have deeper emotions, issues—things they're personally wrestling with but would love to share with the right person that can listen."

She provides positive feedback on the performance of her sexual partners: "They are more experienced here, more feedback how-am-I-doing oriented."

Joy's last sexual encounter rated an impressive 10 out of 10.

When asked if she's tried cybersex, Joy answered: "No need when the real thing is abundant!"

Rory

Rory is a 54 year-old female Technical/Applications/Web Designer. Originally from Washington, DC, Rory describes her single status as "single and swinging." Rory has enjoyed more than 10 dates in the past month, and finds dating in Silicon Valley much easier than other areas.

"The dates are out there ladies," says Rory, "You just have to know how to find and entice the men!"

She has enjoyed sex more than 10 times in the past month, and comments: "The sex partners in Silicon Valley are ab-so-lut-e-ly incredible!"

Rory is a big fan both of online dating and cybersex. Rory comments on online dating: "By meeting your dates online before you meet them in person, you can establish parameters and set expectations with regards to sex."

Rory's experiences with cybersex have been very positive: "With the right partner, it is fan-tast-tic!" Rory's cybersex activities also have led to successful in-person meetings. "Meeting my cybersex partner in person was even better than I imagined! Great connection. We really got to know each other before we met. No secrets. I could tell this man my innermost thoughts, desires, wishes and fantasies. We might have spent years learning as much about each other if we had met any other way."

The most unusual place Rory has enjoyed sex is "on the way home from Hawaii, United First Class, in the restroom. Use your imagination…"

Rory's only experienced one dating disaster after meeting someone online. "I set up a date with a guy who called himself 'TooTall.' He wasn't! He lied about both his height and his age. In addition, he was a pervert! Luckily, we met during broad daylight in a very public place, and I was able to extricate myself from the situation."

She offers these final comments: "If women are sitting around saying men are hard to find… you better believe the men are doing the same thing. Take control of your destiny!!! Try Internet dating! I feel like a kid again… a kid in a candy store! I have met the nicest, kindest, sexiest men in the last 60 days."

The Bad

Not surprisingly, more men (53 percent) than women (37 percent) believe dating in Silicon Valley is more difficult than in other areas. It's that dreaded single-man surplus. According to the 1999 Census Bureau data, there were 5,372 more single men than women aged 20 to 45 in Santa Clara County, the heart of Silicon Valley. Other large metropolitan areas typically have single-men deficits.

While the abundance of men in the Valley is a boon for local women, many men are frustrated, angry and losing hope. As one female survey respondent said, "There are too many hungry men. They're desperate for women, and will take whatever they can get. And that just ain't sexy."

Add to that the 16-hour days spent in a cubicle engineering the next new thing, the faltering economy, the traffic congestion and the high cost of living and, well, it's bad for these guys. Really bad.

But, dating difficulties are not just limited to men. Several of our female interviewees described dating disasters, and great challenges with the Silicon Valley social scene.

Peter

Peter, 27, is a student who has lived in Silicon Valley "almost all my life." He is single and alone, and had just one date in recent months. He ranks Silicon Valley as being "more difficult to get dates" when compared to other areas.

"Women are less friendly here, than in say, San Francisco," says Peter. "There are so many men here, that women don't feel they have to be nice or smart or interesting."

When asked when was the last time he had sex, Peter replied: "What's sex?"

He then went on to elaborate: "My last sexual encounter involved my hand, which made me content, but not fulfilled."

His biggest dating disaster was with a woman "suffering from pot-induced a-motivational syndrome." He describes her as large, "but paradoxically, without any curves. Her shoulders were broad, but her hips were narrower than mine. She also had quite a gut. And no, I did not ask her out on a second date!"

Cathy

Cathy is a student in her early 20's, pursuing a degree in Art. Originally from New England, she has been in the Bay Area less than a year. Cathy finds the dating scene more challenging than back East: "Most of the guys I've met—even the straight ones—are so artificial. They are all about clothes and their damn cell phones. I've pretty much given up any hopes of meeting any real guys out here. But I'm only here until I graduate, so I've settled for casual sex instead. Thank God for craigslist! That's one thing you won't find in a small New Hampshire town."

Cathy says meeting men online takes some getting used to. "First four times it was kind of weird, but you get used to it!"

There's a very important sexual milestone that Cathy has yet to achieve. She describes her dilemma: "The guy I'm dating is seven years older than me, and has lots of stamina. It takes him a long time to finally get off, which leaves me tired and sore, and always unfulfilled. I have yet to have an orgasm—ever."

When asked to describe her ideal sexual experience, Cathy says: "One in which I finally have an orgasm! I don't care where it is or how it happens!"

In lamenting the woes of trying to date in the Valley, many women spoke of Silicon Valley men being afraid to approach women, afraid to even say hello, much less ask a woman out on a date. Some attributed this to the high number of engineers in the area, and the natural tendency of many engineers to be shy, withdrawn types. Others attributed this to lack of social experiences in college, due to male-dominated Engineering classes (not enough interaction with women). Still, others felt the long hours worked by Valley engineers didn't allow them enough opportunities to work on their social and dating skills.

Tara

Tara is a 35 year-old designer, originally from Orange County. She came to the Bay Area two years ago for work. She is currently single.

Tara has tried cybersex, and describes it as "Fun—in a raunchy way."

Tara has a definitive romantic side. Her best sex ever was: "with a guy I was really in love with, in front of the fireplace. It was the way he looked at me."

Tara describes her ideal sexual encounter: "Being completely in love and at ease with each other's bodies, in a nice romantic setting…"

When asked if she had any other comments, Tara asked: "Why are Silicon Valley men so afraid to approach women? They will stare at you all night long and then leave. If you approach them, they become swaggering ego-maniacs and instantly lose every ounce of charm! Say hello, it won't kill you."

Mixed Reviews

Silicon Valley. The name alone once conjured images of tech wizards, instant millionaires, 25 year-old CEOs and money, money, money. Even with a looming recession, the Valley still claims the highest per-capita income in the nation. And while the Internet bust has tarnished its allure, Silicon Valley still draws the best and brightest from other states and around the world.

For those of us that live, work and date here, the Valley is an amazing place; it is still the Valley of the heart's delight, as it was called before the silicon invasion. We are blessed with sunshine 320 days a year. Unemployment is (usually) lower than the national average. We have an abundance of choice; from skiing in Tahoe to surfing in Santa Cruz. The Bay Area is a single person's playground.

So what's not to like?

Well…for starters, in recent years, the glut of instant millionaires drove up the cost of housing, making the Bay Area one of the most expensive places to live in the country. Most of high incomes go towards housing. There's a popular Silicon Valley joke that says: "Only in the Bay area can you make $100,000 a year and still not be able to afford an apartment." If you are single, chances are you have a room-mate…or three. And whomever you're dating has one, too, so privacy is not easy to come by. As for those millionaires—they earned that money by toiling long into the night, every night, along with the rest of us. All of which makes dating a challenge, to say the least.

But, despite these challenges, as these survey respondents have found, good sex—even great sex—is possible, with a little imagination.

Natalie

Natalie is a 24 year-old consultant, who is currently unemployed. Natalie was born and raised in Silicon Valley. She is single, and prefers to meet people the old-fashioned way, rather than through online dating.

Natalie's had one date in the past month, which led to a sexual encounter. Natalie describes the sex: "The guy I had it with is someone I'm seeing on and off, and I think he's the hottest thing. But, it's always the same thing between us. He's a bit on the emotionally unavailable side. But, isn't that why we women love them? The sex itself… it was nice… very intimate because we are comfortable with our bodies regardless. It's always easy for us to pick things up where we left off."

The most unusual place Natalie's had sex is "at my workplace. Very fun. Basically, I had sex on the 36th floor of a San Francisco building, overlooking the Embarcadero."

When asked about her best sex ever, Natalie says: "Hmm… I usually am most aroused when signs of emotional intimacy precede physical intimacy. So, it's less the encounter than what comes before that makes it great sex."

Natalie's biggest dating disaster was with a dot-commer who thought he was King of the World. "I went out for drink with this guy who was so full of himself," says Natalie, "He was one of those 24 year olds who thought he was the smartest thing around. He started his own company and thinks it's the next big thing. Have some humility. And, he was talking to me as if was an old wise man with pearls of wisdom to share. Yuck!"

Natalie offers this final comment on the dating scene: "I hear that San Francisco has the best percentage of singletons out there. But, everyone complains they can't find anyone. Isn't that weird? Why is it so hard to meet people?"

an excerpt from the chapter:
"Chicks Who Prefer Chicks and Other Tales"

The Bay Area has long been known as a haven for same-sex couples seeking sexual freedom and acceptance. Not surprisingly, our survey respondents included a generous mix of same-sex and bisexual couples, sharing their stories and adventures.

Stephanie

Stephanie is 24, single, and loves women. She moved to the Bay Area from Southern California three years ago. She enjoys having sex with her female co-workers, and her most unusual encounter was in the copy room at work.

"Last summer my boss's daughter was working as an intern," Stephanie says, "She was always walking around in tight skirts and low cut blouses. We were working late and she came up to me and asked for help with the copying machine. When I arrived in the copy room, she closed and locked the door. She turned to me, and told me how much she wanted me. We ended up going down on each other, leaning right up against the copy equipment! It was wild!

We ended up having sex through the rest of the summer. She was a fun girl. I hope she decides to do another internship next summer…"

Stephanie says she enjoys being attracted to a woman who at first might seem out of reach, and then "having the woman come on to me."

Stephanie concludes: "Most of the girls in San Francisco and Silicon Valley who you think are straight, are actually totally into girls if given the chance!"

an excerpt from the chapter:
"Unique and Interesting Sex (and other fun things)"

Silicon Valley attracts people of all types, from regions all over the world. Many of the transplants who settle here all have something in common, a spirit of adventure. Those who buy into the stereotype of a cubicle-bound engineer would scoff at the thought of such a person having a spirit of adventure.

But to uproot yourself from familiar surroundings and transplant yourself thousands of miles away where the only person you know is your landlord, takes courage of a special sort. The easiest thing someone can do is stay in the same area where they were born and raised, and just make the best of whatever jobs happen to be available.

The folks who uproot and come to Silicon Valley for jobs—the engineers, sales and marketing folks, web artists and designers—are people of a unique and interesting sort.

The *Sex in Silicon Valley* survey asked all respondents: "What's the most unusual place you've had sex?" This question is always guaranteed to produce some memorable stories. For those who have never had sex in an unusual place, it's bound to get them thinking: "Hmmmm…. I need to try that…" The best of unusual sex stories are featured here, along with a brief profile of their starring performers…

Laurie

Laurie is a 25 year-old consultant, originally from New York. While Laurie describes the people in the Bay Area as "not as friendly and approachable," she is not having any problems with the dating scene. Laurie describes her single status as "single and swinging." She's had seven dates in the past month, and has had sex more than 10 times. When asked to rate the quality of sexual partners out here in the Bay Area, Laurie admits that sex is better than in her native New York. "People like to spice it up out here more," says Laurie.

Laurie's most unusual sexual encounter happened doggy-style at PacBell Park near the statue of Willie Mays. Laurie didn't provide too many details about time of day, or how the encounter came about, but she describes her experience as follows: "It was on the statue in front of PacBell Park. Doggy-style, getting thrusted into, while holding on to the statue of 'Willie' for dear life."

Silicon Valley is notorious for the long hours worked by its many high-tech inhabitants. It's only natural then that the needs of the flesh sometimes get combined with the convenience of the office place.

Jack

Jack is a 28 year-old male, born and raised in California. Jack has worked in San Diego, Fresno and the UK, but most of his career experience has been centered around Silicon Valley. Jack's led a colorful career, starting out as a bike messenger in downtown San Francisco. He holds degrees in medicine and business administration, but comments "neither of my degrees is relevant to my current position."

Jack recently told us about his experiences in the Valley. "I'd been working for this Silicon Valley company for approximately three years.

The first year was the usual—new to the company, no frills stuff—and it went by rather slowly."

Things became more interesting with the arrival of a new co-worker. "One day I spotted a new admin assistant, Judi, down the hall from where I work. Her long blonde hair was more than I could handle, and I kept saying to myself 'only in your dreams.' It was not too long after she started that she began flirting with me. We started spending lunch together just chatting about superficial stuff."

After almost a year of being friends, Jack and Judi became closer. "She started opening up more about her ever unfulfilled libido, and it changed the way I saw her. She was no longer a friend but this girl who had needs to be fulfilled. It was plain to see that her boyfriend was just not taking care of business as he should have been," says Jack.

One day Judi invited Jack to her apartment for lunch. "I thought about it, and I guess I was hoping something would happen. But I would not have been disappointed had it not," he says. After lunch, Judi indulged in a little "smoking therapy" while Jack abstained.

"After a few minutes she started coming onto me, and we had sex on her sofa in the living room where she and her boyfriend would watch TV. I was a little concerned but lost that rather quickly. The sex was incredible," recalls Jack.

Their relationship continued on and off for a good year and they still work together today. "On occasion, we make plans to meet with one another for an evening of fun and that always makes for a less than productive workweek afterwards. The sex is excellent and the fact that we do not have to have a relationship to have this makes it all the more alluring. We usually meet at hotels around the peninsula or down in the south bay," confides Jack.

"Sex definitely makes going to work easier. You can make a dollar and at the same time have fun doing it. In a high-stress work environment, we all need a little release. I feel that the excitement of having sex with co-workers makes up for the lack of excitement in other parts of my life!"

Currently, Jack is involved with a second co-worker. "Sex with co-workers is a lot easier than most people imagine," concludes Jack. "I highly recommend it."

Betty

Betty's best sexual encounter ever occurred with a co-worker. She came out to the Bay Area a year ago for a job opportunity, and found more opportunities than just career advancement.

"The opportunity to physically connect with this co-worker came in a most unlikely place—on the floor of an office in the history building at Stanford University," says Betty. "It was an extremely meditative experience. We were so connected, mentally. As we slid in and out of each other, my entire body felt alive, packed with nerve endings. That was the good part. The bad part was that we were in an uncomfortable and shabby place. I was lying on my back as he pumped into me, and the carpet was very scratchy against my skin, distracting me from some of the pleasure of what was happening. And, once, the janitor came by the door, which temporarily interrupted the flow of what we were doing."

When asked what her ideal sexual experience would be, Betty says: "with someone I totally trust, who understands me, and in a place where there are no scratchy carpets or intrusive janitors."

Tammy

Tammy is a 26 year-old counselor, who was born and raised in Silicon Valley. Tammy is currently in a relationship, and enjoying the sexual aspects of the relationship. "I'd rank our last sexual encounter as an eight. Since we have a good relationship, it wasn't just sex. It was making love, which is much more passionate than just having sex to fulfill a physical urge."

Tammy's most unusual sexual encounter happened with a previous boyfriend. "This guy I was dating worked swing shift at a computer company. I stopped by to see him, and we were both feeling rather...

uh, amorous," says Tammy. "We went into the conference room, closed to the door, and started having sex on the table. That turned out to be rather awkward, so we ended up finishing it on the floor instead. There's something to be said for having sex in an unusual, forbidden, place."

an excerpt from the chapter: "Dating Disasters"

Every survey respondent was asked to include their biggest dating disaster. After reading all these tales of dating woes, it's reassuring to know that everyone's had at least one dating experience they wish they could forget. The important lesson seems to be to pick up the shattered pieces of your dignity, move on, and try again. The lessons learned from today's dating disaster just might lead to tomorrow's dating success. Here are their stories.

"**I WAS AT A COLLEGE** in western Massachusetts where there are five schools within five miles of one another. It was wintertime, and I was invited to a party at the 'jock dorm' of another university by a very cute hockey player boy named Joel (not his real name—actually, I don't remember his real name).

I decided to wear my best tan, slightly baggy pants and leather ankle boots—thank you Madonna for the great fashions you created in the late 80s.

Joel and I were walking towards the dorm, which was downhill from the main campus area. It was already very snowy and cold in New England, and the sidewalks were covered in ice. At some point in our stroll, my little boots hit an ice patch. I've never been a skier, but I somehow managed to stay upright as I slid all the way down the hill. I was screaming, and my arms were flailing, the whole way.

Finally, about 50 feet down the hill, I managed to steer myself into a snow bank, and stop my crazy, runaway slide. I started laughing hysterically with tears rolling down my cheeks. I was laughing so hard that I actually peed on myself. This is not an easy thing to hide in tan pants. When Joel finally caught up with me (some hockey player he was!), I was covered in all things wet—tears, snow and pee.

I told him that I couldn't go to the party, all soaking wet. What did he do? He left me there, alone, and went on to the party without me! I ended up escorting my own wet butt, alone in the night, back to the bus stop for a cold, lonely ride home. The lesson I learned that night was not so much not to pee on myself, but to never go out with a man who won't stand by me if I do."

Jennifer, 30

The Story of the Teenie-Weenie Little Weenie

It seems only logical to include "The Story of the Teenie-Weenie Little Weenie" right after the tales of dating disasters submitted by our readers. This woeful tale was one of the very first stories ever posted to SexinSiliconValley.com, and came from an in-person interview with one of the authors' friends. The incident happened three years ago, and has been infamous in our social circle ever since.

The "Teenie Weenie" story drove many hits to the website, and was voted "best story" in an online poll on the site. The story accounted for the most reader email, with some people amused by the tale, others offended by it.

Here is the complete, unedited Teenie Weenie story, as it appeared on the website. As with all the stories, the names used in the story are pennames to protect the identities of the participants involved, both of whom are still working in the Bay Area.

The True Story of Victoria and Dennis
—better known as "The Story of the Teenie-Weenie Little Weenie"

Victoria recounts her most memorable Silicon Valley sex experience with a shy smile and an embarrassed laugh.

"My first romantic encounter out here was almost enough to make me pack my things and head back East again," Victoria confesses.

Victoria came out to Silicon Valley four years ago. Like most folks, she was lured out with the offer of a high-paying job, pleasant weather and the appeal of the famed California lifestyle.

"Shortly after I arrived, I started dating this guy Dennis, who worked for a famous film company up in the North Bay.

To be honest, I'm not sure now whether I was charmed by the guy, or infatuated with the connections he had to that film company. Dating him made me feel like I was on the inside track of that movie company. He took me on an inside tours of the different company buildings, and even on a tour of one of the world's most famous special effects houses. It was all very, very exciting. We laughed a lot, enjoyed each other's company, and the relationship was going very well until sex came into the picture.

Dennis had one big shortcoming—literally. There was this issue that came between us. An issue of, uh, physical incompatibility."

Victoria laughs nervously, clearing her throat before continuing.

"Okay, so we'd been dating a couple of months, and at first, we'd kept it at kissing and a bit of groping. Things progressed from there, and one day, at his place, we got so heavy into it, I ended up taking off my pants. He got really excited, and stood up to unbutton his jeans. As he was sliding his pants down over his hips, my gaze naturally strayed to his crotch, eagerly looking to see his bulge. (For women, seeing a guy bulging out his pants is a sign we are doing something right.) But, there didn't seem to be any bulge."

Concerned, Victoria wondered if he wasn't erect, and if she didn't excite Dennis enough. His breathing, his caresses and his words indicated he was aroused, but now looking at him, lying next to her in just his black boxers, it looked as if there was nothing there at all—totally flaccid.

"I started kissing him again, as passionately as I knew how, and he began to slide his underwear off. I stopped kissing him so I could fully watch as he removed his boxers. He removed them really, really slowly, trying to be sexy. My eyes were glued to his crotch. For a brief, horrible moment, I wondered if even perhaps he was a flat-chested woman posing as a man, because there just didn't seem to be anything there. I got truly concerned as to what I would see once those boxers finally came all the way off."

To Victoria's relief, Dennis did actually have a penis, but there was one little problem with it.

"I almost gasped out loud when I saw it. Fully erect, it was no larger than my little pinkie. I take that back, I think my little pinkie is longer than his penis. You'd have to see this one to believe it! I reached out to stroke it, thinking that perhaps it wasn't quite all the way erect, and there still might be more yet to come. But no matter how cleverly I stroked, it didn't get any bigger. That's all there was."

Victoria still optimistically proceeded with the lovemaking, reminding herself that size doesn't matter, and thinking perhaps Dennis was an exceptionally skilled lover.

"Perhaps over the years he had learned to compensate for his size with exceptional skill. I mean, after all, it's what you do with what you have that counts, right? Besides, at that point, we were both fully naked and I'd given all the signs I wanted to make love. I didn't feel I could back out then. What could I say: 'Sorry Dennis, I changed my mind because your penis is so small there is no way this encounter is going to be mutually pleasurable.' At that point, I felt like I had to go all the way. "

All the way didn't turn out to be very far. Dennis lay on top of Victoria, kissing her enthusiastically. Victoria spread her legs, and hoped for the best. Dennis pushed himself downward and put his penis inside of her.

"The only way I knew he had entered me, was by looking down at where our bodies joined. I didn't feel a thing," said Victoria. "I'd hoped I'd feel at least a little something! I wrapped my legs up around him, hoping to take him further into me. I wanted to at least feel something. I really did want this to work between us. That's when it happened. He slipped out. He was so small, he simply slipped out.

I guided him back in, thinking it was just a fluke, and he promptly fell out again. He'd pump a few strokes, fall out, then pump some more. He didn't think this was odd at all. In no time at all, he came, and then fell asleep almost instantly.

I rolled over, and he slid out in a slippery mess, but to add insult to injury, the condom was no longer attached to his now even tinier shriveled little thing. So I had to reach inside myself, and fish out the used condom. I was disgusted, and thought that if he was bigger, maybe he would at least fit properly into a condom!

I just lay there for like ten minutes, staring at his shriveled little thing and resenting it. First of all, the condom incident. Okay, like he could have had the decency to hold on to the condom, pull out and dispose of it before dropping off into dreamland. But, now there was another problem. Because the condom had slipped off with fresh sperm in it, I now had to contend with the worry that his sperm was now swimming all over my female parts, searching for a nice egg to fertilize.

And, even more than that, I was I completely sexually frustrated from the whole experience. The fact that he slipped out time and time again made me feel wide—totally slutty—and I have never been promiscuous. My previous boyfriend had always commented how tight I felt. Feeling wide and too loose was a new, and most unpleasant, feeling."

Despite the awkward evening, Victoria still tried to make the best of the relationship. Figuring sex wasn't everything, she strived to focus on Dennis' other good qualities.

"Dennis was definitely a nice guy, and will make someone a fine husband someday—someone he is physically and emotionally compatible with—but that someone isn't me."

After six months of dating, Victoria broke up with Dennis.

"I'd tried to make the relationship work, I really did. I even briefly wondered about penile implants. I knew I wanted children someday, and maybe there was some sort of implant that could at least make him big enough so we could fit together long enough to conceive a child. I was willing to be flexible about the whole size thing, but perhaps it was his size that led to his other insecurities.

"It was much more than just the sex thing. He became very clingy and I felt completely suffocated. I no longer had a life of my own. He thought our sex life was great and wanted to make love all the time. For me, it was dreadfully boring and I contemplated stapling reading material to the ceiling so I'd have something to do while he slipped in and out, in and out. After a while, it all just got to be way too much. While I still admired the many good qualities that had made us friends in the first place, I had to end our relationship as lovers. It was just too much to take anymore. I found myself avoiding his phone calls, dreading his visits, and breathing a vast sigh of relief when he went home and I had my apartment to myself again.

I wanted to remain friends, but for him, it was either boyfriend-and-girlfriend, or nothing. If I didn't want to date him, he didn't want anything to do with me.

I sure wish him well. I actually feel sorry for him. In a society that unfairly equates manliness with penis size, poor Dennis has the endowment of a Chihuahua.

I'm betting he hasn't had a lot of sex in his lifetime. He's not someone you'd go back to for seconds. A woman needs to feel somewhat tight and virginal every time she is with her man. With Dennis, I felt as wide as the Grand Canyon."

0-595-23895-5

www.ingramcontent.com/pod-product-compliance
Lightning Source LLC
Chambersburg PA
CBHW020250290526
45784CB00003B/1190